Palgrave Studies in Impact Finance

The *Palgrave Studies in Impact Finance* series provides a valuable scientific 'hub' for researchers, professionals and policy makers involved in Impact finance and related topics. It includes studies in the social, political, environmental and ethical impact of finance, exploring all aspects of impact finance and socially responsible investment, including policy issues, financial instruments, markets and clients, standards, regulations and financial management, with a particular focus on impact investments and microfinance.

Titles feature the most recent empirical analysis with a theoretical approach, including up to date and innovative studies that cover issues which impact finance and society globally.

More information about this series at
http://www.palgrave.com/gp/series/14621

Daniel Cash

Sustainability Rating Agencies vs Credit Rating Agencies

The Battle to Serve the Mainstream Investor

palgrave
macmillan

Daniel Cash
Aston University
Birmingham, UK

ISSN 2662-5105 ISSN 2662-5113 (electronic)
Palgrave Studies in Impact Finance
ISBN 978-3-030-71692-9 ISBN 978-3-030-71693-6 (eBook)
https://doi.org/10.1007/978-3-030-71693-6

Cover credit: Henrik Sorensen

This Palgrave Macmillan imprint is published by the registered company Springer Nature Switzerland AG
The registered company address is: Gewerbestrasse 11, 6330 Cham, Switzerland

Contents

CHAPTER 1

Introduction

In reading the title of this book, you would be forgiven for thinking 'what battle?' The ESG rating agencies, and the credit rating agencies, are two different industries. Though colloquially adjoined by the concept of *rating*, they serve two different purposes. The credit rating agencies serve to assess the creditworthiness of an entity and if ESG issues are of *material* relevance, then they should be considering those issues as well as financial issues. The ESG rating agencies exist to consider the sustainability of an entity, and then rate/rank it accordingly. In the light of the potential 'mainstreamisation' of the sustainable investor movement, there is increasing business being sent the way of the ESG rating agencies. However, there have since been a number of research endeavours that have identified key flaws in the delivery of those ESG-related ratings, which is calling into question the suitability of those agencies to meet this new demand.

The notion of a 'battle' between these two industries to serve this new mainstream investor base is not widely considered, but it has been identified. An interesting article in the *Financial Times* in 2019, entitled 'credit rating agencies join battle for ESG supremacy' suggested that:

> A flurry of dealmaking has begun among firms that provide companies with environmental, social and governance ratings, fed by increasing demand for the data among investors and regulators. The sector has traditionally been dominated by index providers such as MSCI and a handful of specialist

D. Cash, *Sustainability Rating Agencies vs Credit Rating Agencies*, Palgrave Studies in Impact Finance,
https://doi.org/10.1007/978-3-030-71693-6_1

> firms, such as Sustainalytics. Now Moody's and S&P Global, two of the big three credit rating agencies, are elbowing their way in, offering separate ESG scores on companies in addition to their traditional assessments of creditworthiness.[1]

The article continued by discussing how the market for ESG information is growing all the time, and that the credit rating agencies are well aware of this. Whilst a number of aspects would need to be added to the credit rating agencies' offerings, it was very much suggested that the two industries would come into contact at some point for the lucrative rewards that awaited them for adjoining to the movement of sustainable investment.

It is always wise to write a book like this, as if the reader is uninitiated with the world of credit ratings, because it is a somewhat niche element of the financial sector even though its impact came to light massively in the Financial Crisis. Nevertheless, this article in the FT made me wonder of what may affect that battle, and how it would play out—that is what this book is built on. In order to examine these questions further, we shall embark upon a journey that considers the development of the 'mainstreamisation' of the concept of sustainable investment, the histories and trajectories of the two industries, the underlying dynamics of the rating relationship, and then after reviewing the regulatory developments in the area of non-financial informational disclosure, we shall conclude with an assessment of who is likely to win this 'battle' that has been predicted.

The mainstreamisation of the concept of investing in a responsible and sustainable way is well under way. It is a direct response to the Financial Crisis and the actions of market participants who prioritised short-termism and an apparently blind faith in third-party verifiers of credit risk. The movement aims to force investors to consider elements of ESG—Environmental, Social, and Governance factors—into their decision making, which has the hope of forcing issuers to rise to the challenge also attached to it. The movement has been progressing, but is hitting snags along the way not that the leading investors are starting to turn their attention to it. On significant snag is the flow of information. From the issuers, investors want higher quality information. From the third-parties like ESG rating agencies and credit rating agencies, the investors want that higher quality information to be as standardised as possible, so that performance over industries and regions can be compared. As we shall see, there have been a number of initiatives developed that want to bring these requests to fruition, but they are also finding significant problems along the way. Now, with the E.U. and the U.S. taking very different approaches, there is even more divergence on the global scene and divergence is precisely what the investors do not want.

To assist with these issues, the ESG rating agencies and credit rating agencies are being challenged by a variety of initiatives to step up and provide solutions. Global initiatives like the Principles for Responsible Investment (PRI) have aligned themselves with the credit rating agencies to encourage them to a. increase their dialogue with investors and then b. provide more of what the investors require. This is underway and as we shall see in Chapter 3, the credit rating agencies are purposively and decisively turning their attention towards this nascent but potentially lucrative market. For the ESG rating agencies, their relatively younger market is attempting to cope with the pressures that come with serving the mainstream, and it is running into difficulties. How they handle the pressure that is building in the market for them will fundamentally determine the future of their industry, because the presence of much bigger market players suggests that if they do not get it right, their industry will not survive to tell the story. Therefore, in Chapter 2, we shall look at the industry, clear up some terminological problems in the literature, and then seek to understand better the chances of the industry overcoming the difficulties that have been identified.

In Chapter 4, we shall embark upon a really deep excavation of the 'rating dynamic' as I call it. Whether in relation to the ESG rating agency dynamic or the credit rating dynamic, there are fundamental truths that affect the balance between the parties and to have a hope of predicting who may prevail out of this prophesied battle it is important to know how that dynamic works. There are key elements, such as the need to 'signal', reduce competitive pressures, and extract the benefits from an oligopolistic model that need to be considered, and we shall do that. This leads us to the final chapter which will first present the regulatory and cultural developments in both the U.S. and the E.U. These two entities have been chosen because one is the home of the majority of these rating entities, and the other is attempting to lead the world in issues of sustainability and also disclosure. Other entities are worth mentioning of course, like China, but their relationships with the credit rating entities are much newer, less developed, and impacted by a whole host of different issues (like political models, etc.) Once that is established, we shall consider some private initiatives before then concluding with analysing some potential scenarios that may take effect, and then decide which is the more likely to come to pass.

The ESG rating agencies are under pressure, and the credit rating agencies are joyfully adding to it. The rewards for aligning oneself to this market could be momentous, and the market knows it. The trajectory of the two industries has been stark recently, with the ESG rating agencies needing to defend their practices and the potential of forthcoming regulatory frameworks for the first time in their history, whilst the credit rating agencies have consolidated since the Crisis and are going 'full steam ahead' towards this new and exciting marketplace for them. However, they themselves are constrained, and these constraints are constantly on the mind of the rating agencies, i.e. liability. The credit rating agencies are acutely aware of *any* potential liability that they are exposed to, and that fear is real in this new market given that they will have to espouse their opinion more than they usually do. But, for the ESG rating agencies, the prospect of the market or a region cracking the code on either a. increasing the informational flow in the market, or better still b. standardising the disclosure of that information, provide it with a glimmer of hope that they can develop their own credit rating industry-like trajectory and become powerhouses themselves. The next few years will really bring these two contrasting developments into focus and, potentially, into conflict. What we need to do is consider how that may look, why it will be, and what the outcome may be.

Note

1. Billy Nauman, 'Credit Rating Agencies Join Battle for ESG Supremacy' (2019) *Financial Times* (Sept 17). https://www.ft.com/content/59f60306-d671-11e9-8367-807ebd53ab77 (accessed 04/01/2021).

CHAPTER 2

The 'Mainstreaming' of Responsible Investment

The Financial Crisis, an event which defined the lives of so many, is righty seen as an incredibly negative moment in recent history. Livelihoods were ruined, economies crashed, and large swathes of society have been living with the financial repercussions ever since. Furthermore, the era was to become a seedbed for a political revolution that saw Donald Trump elected to the Office of President of the U.S., whilst on the other side of the Atlantic Ocean the British electorate decided to leave the European Union. Infighting within the E.U. sprouted in the wake of the upheaval, with populist governments springing up in places like Hungary. Now, the E.U. is pursuing a less-is-more approach as the bloc enters unchartered territory with its authority on the line. In the East, China continues to flex its political muscles in the region, backed by an ever-growing economy and an expansive foreign policy that has seen the Belt-and-Road initiative continue to grow. Political hot potatoes like the governance of Hong Kong have been handled in an authoritarian manner, all amidst a global trade war with the U.S. In the U.S., the country has been gripped by social upheaval in the wake of a number of high-profile killings of black men and women at the hands of police. Then, almost a century after the outbreak of the so-called Spanish Flu, the world has been engulfed by the COVID-19 'Coronavirus'. This virus has led to the world, essentially, being 'locked down' with the consequence being that economic, political, and overarching social divisions and problems have become heightened

D. Cash, *Sustainability Rating Agencies vs Credit Rating Agencies*, Palgrave Studies in Impact Finance,
https://doi.org/10.1007/978-3-030-71693-6_2

for all to see. However, the Financial Crisis did initiate a movement that has continued at a rapid pace and is beginning to impact upon the 'mainstream' financial arena; that movement was to make modern finance more 'responsible'.

Making modern finance more 'responsible' arguably makes sense in the wake of what I have described above. Seeking to make modern finance consider more than just the potential financial return from their actions, or seeking to expand the time horizons that are considered in financial circles, simply makes a lot of sense when we consider what caused the Financial Crisis. However, and unsurprisingly, things are not that simple. When I say 'financial arena', what do I mean? Are there particular targets for this movement, or is the aim to change the wider *culture*? When I say that an aim is to increase the time horizons which are considered, then how long should one aim for? How long is *material* for effective decisions to be made for financial entities? If the aim is to make modern finance consider more than just the potential return, then what should they consider? Should said considerations be externally mandated, or should financial entities be allowed to develop their own understanding of what should be considered? Would allowing financial entities to choose, be the most efficient approach, and would those entities even want that freedom? As you can clearly see, this issue is extraordinarily complex. Even more so, what if the *aim* was not even agreed upon! What if we did not even have a standardised definition for the movement we want to develop? Unfortunately, this is absolutely the case. As it is not my intention to contribute to that complexity, I would like to digress for a moment and look at the importance of clarifying, definitionally, what we are looking at in this book.

2.1 Definitional Complexity and the Origins of the Movement

The history of investing for a reason other than purely for financial gain is a long and storied one. We will look more at this history in the next subsection, but there are a few definitions that get used in the literature and wider financial arena that may confuse. For example, there appears to be a consistent and common interconnecting usage of the terms 'Socially Responsible Investment' and 'Responsible Investment'. Furthermore, there are many occasions were 'sustainable finance' is used, and then occasions were 'responsible finance' is used to describe the *movement* we are concerned with in this book. There are a variety of reasons for this and, for better or worse, this issue is probably emblematic of the anchor that is holding the movement back (relatively speaking). Krosinsky and Robins explain this neatly when they say that:

> ...it's necessary to provide some guidance on the terminology used in this book. Over the past 30 years, a range of terms, notably "social", "ethical", "green", "responsible", "socially responsible" and "sustainable", have been used to describe the merging practice of incorporating extra-financial factors within investment decision-making. One woman's "ethical investing" is another man's "socially responsible investing", and one firm's "responsible investing" is another manager's "sustainable investing". On reflection, this embarrassment of semantic richness is perhaps understandable for a rapidly evolving approach, where the final form has yet to be settled. In such a fluid field, we are all well aware of the dangers of false precision.[1]

Ballestero et al. discuss how 'SRI, also known as ethical investing, responsible investing, green investing, impact investing or sustainable investing, shares with conventional investing the top priority given to financial profitability, while considering in additional social, ethical or environmental parameters'.[2] Yet, Hebb tells us that 'responsible investing has always had a broad mandate. Put simply, it is a long-term sustainable investment strategy that values environmental, social, and governance factors in the public equities portfolios of investors concerned with the long term risks that ESG considerations may pose'.[3] One includes the 'S' of 'socially', whilst one drops it; but is this important? Cullis et al. state that:

> The terms *ethical* and *socially responsible* (and, more commonly nowadays, *sustainable*) are labels regularly attached to a range of enterprises; it is important to ask what these terms mean (besides indicating that the activity is generally a good thing). *Social Responsibility* is the favoured term... there more troublesome label of *ethical* having been dropped. But could this legitimisation of SRI as part of "third way" politics lead to a watering down of the ethical brew? CSR has formed a broad agenda where businesses are asked to improve their social, environmental, and local economic impact and consider how businesses affect society at large in terms of human rights, social cohesion, fair trade, and corruption. If anything, the notion of sustainability is even more vague and ell-embracing.[4]

The authors continue by stating that 'it seems that the popularity of what we might now best refer to as SRI (the internationally most favoured label) is set to continue to rise, given its increased visibility to institutional investors and because around 70 percent of individual investors feel they ought to be investing ethically even if they are not doing so at present'.[5] It is tempting to agree with them, that SRI is the most favoured label, but there is no definitive evidence for this. Actually, I would argue that *Responsible Investment* is the most agreed-upon term, solely because of the popularity and the acceptance of the PRI, otherwise known as the *Principles for Responsible Investment*, which is a UN-backed global initiative that has over 1000 of the world's leading investors and financial entities as partners (we shall be introduced to the PRI in much more detail shortly). Yet, as ever, there are major issues with these definitions so far. One is that the PRI, in spite of their primacy, have been criticised for being a 'misleading indicator' because 'the reality is that PRI signatories commit only to behaving in accordance with a set of principles for responsible investment, a commitment that falls well short of integrating ESG considerations into all of their investment decisions'.[6] The second issue is an issue I have with the focus of the definitions of socially responsible investment, or responsible investment, is that it is merely focused on the actions of the investor. Whilst it is absolutely understandable that the investor has been identified as being the lynchpin in the development of the movement (which I agree with), the definition does not take into account, directly, the role of those investors invest in. Perhaps I am splitting hairs and that, in reality, the act of the investor taking a 'responsible approach' to their investing, i.e. considering more than just financial performance, and/or a longer time-horizon, has the effect of forcing the issuer to alter their processes as well. I digress. Potentially, on that basis, it may be more appropriate to talk of 'sustainable finance' because, as Miles describes:

> Although there is no comprehensive definition, the concept of sustainable finance encompasses the lending and investment activities of private equity financiers and institutional investors, as well as entities from the public sector such as the World Bank and multilateral development banks. At its broadest, sustainable finance refers to the "mainstreaming of environmental and socio-economic criteria into lending, investment and other financial services". The NGO community tends to interpret it as requiring more

> innate changes in approach, such as deep-rooted commitment to social and environmental responsibility, transparency, accountability, and precaution.[7]

Rather than complicate the issue any further, it may be best to focus on the broader objective of the movement, whether funnelled through the investor or not, and Robins gives us a clear definition upon which we can build when he says that 'part of the essence of contemporary sustainable investing is the realisation that investors need to understand, measure, and promote superior financial *and* non-financial performance'.[8]

Just a moment ago, we saw the criticism of the PRI in that it does not force its signatories to *integrate* a concept known as 'ESG' more into their financial processes, but what does that all mean? 'ESG' stands for environment, social, and governance and relates to aspects that should be considered when decided on, say, investment opportunities. Examples may include the impact a business has upon the climate (for the 'E'), the business' position with regard to modern slavery, or its record on employee-related issues (for the 'S'), or the strength and consistency of its Board and internal management structure (for the 'G'). However, we can see an issue in my describing of 'ESG', because for the 'S' I mentioned the imagined business' approach to modern slavery; what if there are (and there predominantly are in the developed world) strict regulations governing the exploitation of people? Abiding by those rules, and making sure the company proactively and efficiently declares such adherence, may fall under the 'G'overnance aspect too. The variety and multiplicity of the world and everything in it mean that ESG, as a concept, is a really good starting point but, in reality, it needs to be contextualised and understood on a variety of levels, all the time.

Nevertheless, even if that definitional complexity is somehow resolved, how the concept of ESG came to be, and how it is applied, simply continues the complexity. Let us start with a simple question. So far, we have seen many explanations and definitions of the *movement* of encouraging financial players to think about and, moreover, start to act upon the premise that one can participate in the market and think of something else other than financial return. We have also seen that the emphasis has been placed upon the 'investor'. However, who *is* this investor? What is their position? Understanding this means we *may* be able to ascertain what they want from the interaction and, perhaps more crucially, what they can *do*. To deviate for one moment, in the wake of the Wall Street Crash of 1929 and the subsequent Great Depression, the focus was on protecting the so-called retail investor—the woman or man who participated in the marketplace—because they were deemed to require such protection in the face of a corporate curtain that they quite often fell victim to. Modern corporate law across the world has been built on that premise. However, as Coffee insightfully describes '...that is the past. The era in which retail investors "owned" companies or moved the trading markets is long gone and "deader than disco". Today, retail investors account for only a modest minority of the ownership of large, publicly traded companies and probably only between 2 and 4% of the trading in NYSE-listed companies. Stock ownership is now dominated by institutional investors, who are increasingly diversified and often indexed'.[9] Whilst there may be cultural stimuli that alter that ratio between jurisdictions, it is likely to be representative of the modern western world. We will look at this fascinating development in much more detail in Chapter 4, but there are so many questions that this understanding rightly raises, like what does that diversified approach mean to the act of considering something other than financial return (?), are institutional investors legally allowed to consider something else other than financial return (?), and what does that mean for the interaction between investor and company? The last question is particularly relevant when we understand that there are now three major institutional investors—the so-called Big Three of BlackRock, State Street, and Vanguard—who between them, by themselves, and with the help of smaller players (who will often just follow the market leaders), have the capability to *force* a company to take particular actions, if not apply the heaviest of pressure to a Board of a public company. Whilst these questions are fascinatingly important, for us at this stage of the chapter, the main question to ask is what does this concentration and market position mean for the investing options available to the larger investment players?

There are a variety of investing options within the world of 'responsible investment'. Our focus in this book is on the 'mainstreaming' of the *movement* and, in that sense, there is a preferred approach and for a particular reason. However, to understand why that approach is favoured, we must understand the other approaches and the development of them. The concept of investing and partaking in financial action for anything other than financial gain, and in whatever ratio, i.e. how much one *does* in relation to how much they *gain*, is unsurprisingly rooted in religious history. The Catholic Church forbade loans with interest attached in the Middle Ages,[10] which was an approach that had been appropriated from the

Islamic world.[11] Ballestero et al. rightly discuss how the Catholic Church, in forbidding the attachment of interest (with Emperor Charlemagne, for example, declaring in the eighth century that the practice was illegal), 'not only financed social investment with their income, but also canalised a significant flow of rents to hospitals, nursing homes and schools'.[12] What the authors do not mention is that this process was about societal control, and directly led to the development of Protestantism led by Martin Luther—the Church became, in essence, the only corporation in the market—[13] but I digress. In other examples of religiously-inspired investment practices, the Quakers were well known to advise their members to invest with a social criteria in mind, particularly based around concepts of peace, brotherhood, and solidarity; this is known to have inspired similar ideals across Italy, Spain, and other European countries in the seventeenth and eighteenth centuries. Moving forward, the Quakers were a component of 'ethical investors' that inhabited the British investing scene (collectively known as 'Church Investors'), with the 'Church' developing investment portfolios that had specific ethical constraints on what could be invested in, and what could not. Their approach then (and which continues to be the case) was one of exclusion or, as we would say today, the application of a 'negative screen', i.e. certain stocks could not be invested in, usually the so-called sin stocks like alcohol, tobacco, defence, and gambling-related stocks. Whilst the UK has been a pioneer in certain areas—such as the development of the ethical research service EIRIS in 1983 (more on them in the next chapter)—the so-called quiet period between the Second World War and the 1980s represents the seedbed for what has subsequently developed. For example, the first ethical fund developed in Europe was the *Asnvar Aktiefond Sverige* fund in Sweden in 1965, created by the Swedish Church, but the Vietnam War really became the catalyst of what was to come. In response to a massive groundswell of negative sentiment towards both the war itself, but particularly how it was conducted, American students began to push for change and focused on the companies that supported the war—divestment in associated companies became commonplace. The same approach was taken against South Africa for its implementation of the Apartheid system. In the modern era, now private enterprises started to have more of an impact too, with entities such as Triodos in the Netherlands, or Banca Etica in Italy, taking an active role on the commitment to social and financial returns.

However, the 1980s and the decades that followed saw the first globalised efforts to take action within the 'responsible finance' diaspora. A number of UN Conferences were put together to focus on multinational responses to issues stemming from human impact upon the climate, starting with the UN Conference on the Human Environment in 1972, held in Stockholm. In 1992, the UN Conference on Environment and Development was held in Rio de Janeiro, with the World Summit on Sustainable Development being held in Johannesburg in 2002. Ten years later, the UN Conference on Sustainable Development was held in Rio de Janeiro, again, in 2012 with the most recent being held in New York, labelled the UN Sustainable Development Summit in 2015. You can see from the above that, at a certain point, the concept of 'sustainable development' becomes central to the mission of the globalised entity. That concept was popularised and defined by the so-called Brundtland Report, which was a report developed by the World Commission on Environment and Development in 1987, led by former Norwegian Prime Minister Gro Harlem Brundtland. The Commission declared that sustainable finance 'is finance that meets the social, environmental, and livelihood needs of the present generation without compromising the ability of future generations to meet their own needs and that creates a fair balance between societies in the north and the south'.[14] What the Commission did was to place the responsibility squarely at the feet of 'finance' as an industry. However, as Weber notes, 'a general strategy as to how the financial sector might contribute to sustainable development is missing'.[15]

The consequences of not having a defined and agreed-upon strategy in place were brutally witnessed during the Financial Crisis of 2007/08. With developed economies grinding to a halt, all on the basis of short-termism, increased financialisation, and ultimately the development of the concept of financial entities being 'too-big-to-fail', the potential of that era being a turning point emerged. Hebb talks of the Financial Crisis revealing:

> the critical need for greater oversight of today's financial markets. In the aftermath of the Financial Crisis institutional investors are increasingly realising that while much of this oversight will occur through government regulation, increasingly large institutional investors are being called upon to provide this type of active engagement and ownership in our capital markets. The result is not the institutional investor "socialism" envisioned by Peter Drucker, but rather a reconfigured capitalism crafted by these enormous financial pools. Many institutional investors are using their influence to engage and in some cases aggressively challenge the management

> of corporations in order to improve the environmental, social and governance (ESG) standards of the firms in which they invest. Such activity, known as responsible investment (RI), seeks long-term shareholder value for future beneficiaries.[16]

Thus, the Financial Crisis became a 'trigger'[17] that initiated a sea-change in direction within the financial markets. Now, the focus was on how to make the financial arena are more longer-termed and more contributory affair. To that end, the market had, and still has, a number of options available to them. Krosinsky and Purdom helpfully categorise these options into what they label as the 'seven tribes' of responsible investment.[18] In no particular order, they are:

- 'Values First'—this approach is the one based upon religious values, traditionally. The common approach within this 'tribe' is to apply negative screens to exclude investment opportunities that do not fit into one's 'value-driven' mandate, like 'sin' stocks.
- 'Value First'—this approach involved 'using ESG as among primary considerations' when investing, although it is different to 'ESG integration' as we shall see below. The sentiment here is that investors will invest for financial return, but use methods which can have an additional societal effect.
- Community/Impact—the focus for this approach is on intentionality. 'Impact Investing' is a phrase coined by the Rockefeller Foundation and this explains the sentiment, in that it is often a Foundation/charitable endeavour designed to improve a given community or people.
- Thematic Investing—this approach involves focusing on a particular sector within which one will invest, with something like renewable energy or electric vehicle production being an example amongst many.
- Engagement/Advocacy—this approach involved shareholders *actively* engaging with both companies and policymakers on an array of issues that can have 'positive externalities', like compensation, tax, regulation, and so on. The authors note how such engagement is rarely publicised, so as to encourage further engagement with the target.
- Norms-based Screening—this approach entails using an external, and often global standard as a minimum for investment. This has

been explained as 'investing that excludes companies (or government debt) from a portfolio on account of any failure by the issuer to meet internationally accepted norms such as the UN Global Compact, the Kyoto Protocol or the UN Declaration of Human Rights, etc'.[19]
- ESG Integration—conducted by analysts, asset managers, and investors, this approach involved utilising ESG data from internal but often third-party informational providers to enrich the investment decision-making process.

It is interesting to note that the scholars champion the 'value-first' approach as the approach which could have the largest societal impact, but admit themselves that 'interest in factoring ESG considerations into investment itself is at record levels'. This is because, as the scholars continue, 'arguably, the first waves of socially responsible investing were implemented too soon, were at times too politically focused, and attempted to use poor to non-existent data…'. What is interesting here are two things in particular. First, the development of 'ESG' and its mainstream usage, theoretically speaking, was developed to gently persuade an extremely hesitant financial sector. The financial sector was comfortable with the concept of analysing and integrating data that was concerned with the governance of the entities they were investing in/exposed to, but as Coffee tells us, 'to bring SRI investing into the mainstream, something had to be done… conceptually, they "rebranded" SRI investing and converted it into ESG investing by asserting that consideration of the "governance factors" associated with public corporations would enable the fiduciary to identify superior investment and enhance risk-adjusted return'. He continues by stating that 'necessity is often the mother of invention, and the modest claim advanced is merely that the need to calm the fears of risk averse trustees best explains the addition of "governance" factors to environmental and social ones in order to convert SRI into ESG'.[20] We shall examine the legal consequences that must be considered for investment managers in institutional investors who, as we know, essentially *are* the modern-day market later in Chapter 4, but this idea of lawyers changing the definitional landscape to allow risk-averse managers to partake in investment opportunities makes sense. The second aspect that is interesting is that, as you will hopefully agree once you finish reading this book, the environment that prevented the 'first waves' of socially responsible investment from taking hold still exist today; the terminology may have been altered to please the risk-averse, but the environment has not changed at all. What do I mean by this? Well, I am foreshadowing a lot of the book here, but the concept of the implementation of SRI being too politically focused is massively relevant today, with the E.U. trying to force the concept on the market and the U.S. forcing the market to reject the principle. The construct of what we are discussing in this book has, arguably, been implemented well before the necessary infrastructure has been established, with a clear example being the target of this book—third-party informational providers. If the market was poor then and the result was that poor data was being utilised to no positive effect, then we shall see in this book that nothing has really changed; the Sustainability Rating Agencies, and the Credit Rating Agencies, are both a. being massively criticised for a lack of informational value in their products, and b. simultaneously complaining of the lack of nutritious information available within the marketplace with which they could make informed decisions with. Changing the definition does not change the reality.

2.2 'Mainstreamisation' and ESG Integration

Nevertheless, the integration of ESG into the investment processes of large investment vehicles is becoming the dominant approach for the 'mainstreamisation'[21] of the concept of responsible investment. As we saw earlier from Coffee, the emphasis since the Financial Crisis has been on finding a new form of finance that is both a. practicable for, and palatable to the financial marketplace, and b. allows for the development of the sustainable agenda. In truth, the previous sentence is essentially the classic battle that we are seeing at present, and there are many hurdles to clear before the two aspects are synergistically brought together. However, that has not stopped the juggernaut from moving forward. Lubin and Esty consider this move as a 'megatrend'. They qualify this view on the basis that, over the past decade or so, such issues as those categorised under ESG have encroached upon all areas of business so that they now focus on creating 'value for customers, shareholders, and other stakeholders'.[22] Speaking specifically about the 'E' component, they note how the geopolitical climate is changing because rising powers like China and India have intensified competition for natural resources, whilst 'externalities' such as carbon dioxide emissions and water usage are increasingly becoming more 'material' to businesses the world over. The growth of the concept of ESG and its incorporation into the investment decision-making process has been substantial, and one need not look for long for arguments that suggest it will soon become the standard approach, even against conventional return-only investment approaches; PwC predict, for example, that ESG-based funds in Europe will triple by 2025 to be worth more than €7.6tn.[23]

Pinney et al. suggest, interestingly, that there are several factors that are driving the development of ESG integration within mainstream investment practices. The first they note is the increase in female and millennial investors, who are becoming more active in the decisions regarding *how* the investment process is undertaken.[24] There are a number of reasons as to the proliferation of female investors and their growing impact on the investing process, with the growth of female investment managers and business leaders being suggested as an important component. Subsequently, it has also been suggested that women may be more risk-averse than their male counterparts, which means investment managers either a. pursuing their investment, or b. under close scrutiny from their investor base, are having to *signal* to their investor base that they are considering more elements in order to potentially reduce the riskiness of the procedure.[25] A second major contributor is the growing realisation that 'ESG is a viable way to increase alpha and manage risk across their portfolios'. The third is that there has been a marked growth is what the scholars call multi-stakeholder initiatives (like the PRI) established with the aim of resolving inherent hurdles that exist in the mainstreaming of the concept. The last element the scholars identify is the development of new technologies designed to streamline the process and make it more efficient. They discuss how advances in AI and data science have allowed for the development of sophisticated algorithms that allow for a number of approaches to be taken; one example cited is 'smart-scraping', which is an automated process whereby machine learning technologies allow for company reports to be 'scraped' for any relevant ESG-related information and then fed into the larger quantitative processes. Whilst the growth is impressive, it is perhaps worth returning to the sentiment that started the chapter and asks what is it exactly that is growing? You have read so far phrases such as 'ESG integration', 'responsible investing', and 'value-first investing', but what is the context to all of this?

The reality is that the market will only be dictated to as far as it is willing to listen. This is problematic for traditionalists who believe that the ethos of sustainability should be *enforced*; those traditionalists are finding that the reality of the situation is much different to the idealised versions of potential events that they have been hoping for. Again, the following is foreshadowing a much more detailed analysis that we will undertake in Chapter 4, but the concept of *enforcing* this sustainability agenda must be done through regulators. What we are seeing currently is regulators having to realise that it is the market that gets what it wants, not onlookers or theorists. For example, Revelli argues that 'to return to the heart of the game, ethics must play a leading role in the change of financial practices, including at the investment level. The principle is to reintegrate finance within ethics, not ethics within finance'.[26] Is Revelli wrong in his proclamation? Whether one agrees or not, the reality is that finance is only interested in integrating non-financial considerations into its practices as long as they are 'material'. Interestingly, Revelli questions whether this is because of intent, or because the change is simply too radical an idea for the traditionalist or conventional economists. In discussing the literature on the topic of SRI, he notes that 'the vast majority of published research in this area describes empirical testing of SRI data with the sole purpose of demonstrating whether SRI is profitable and less risky than conventional investments'. This is a fascinating question, because the implication is that economic theory and academe is actively seeking to kowtow to 'finance', rather than objectively assess the validity of the approach. Or, is it the case that the world just understands that finance, with its traditions, will be unlikely to adopt a new approach if it is not framed within parameters that they understand? Traditionally, the sole purpose of the investor and the corporation has been to generate profit, so placing that at the very centre of the conversation with regard to responsible finance may be the best approach. It is all very debatable. For Revelli, he is emphatic when he states that the vast amount of research into the validity of responsible finance is based upon the theoretical foundation that emanated from the Chicago School and neoliberal theory, whose most famous proponent Friedman argued, in 1970, that 'corporate social responsibility' (as the concept of taking financial action for any reason other than financial return was known then) was a constraint on the profit maximisation of the corporation, which should be its most cherished purpose.[27]

Returning to the concept of 'materiality', it has been noted in the literature that, traditionally, anything ESG-related has been regarded as being an 'externality'. Now however, there is an ever-growing body of research that suggests that integrating ESG considerations into one's practice can reduce one's risk, and even add value over time, although there is research that also paints a less positive picture of the evolution of non-financial data and its importance.[28] This research that purports to demonstrate the potential of ESG integration labels this phenomenon the 'business case',[29] which perhaps backs Revelli's argument. The 'business case' was perhaps enshrined at the turn of the century, when banks began to create internal departments that we tasked with providing responsible finance-related data; this is particularly relevant as banks like Unibanco in Brazil, and the global HSBC, added these offerings to their sell-side brokerages so that they were not exposing the universe of their investor base to such considerations, not just 'responsible investors'.[30]

ESG integration has been described as consisting of taking certain ESG criteria into account in conventional financial management, 'or making ESG available to all management teams, or encouraging cooperation between financial and non-financial analysts', Furthermore, 'ESG integration practices cover large amounts of assets under management but are less restrictive than SRI', which has led to the practice being labelled as more 'inclusionary' than other approaches such as the 'best-in-class' or 'best-effort' approaches.[31] The PRI explain how the integration of ESG may take place, when they affirm that it may include practitioners: analysing ESG information generally; identifying material financial and ESG factors; assessing the potential impact of material factors on economic, country, sector, or company performance; and making investment decisions that include considerations of all material factors. What we can deduct here is that it is all rather vague, and that may be intentional to allow for the greatest amount of flexibility for practitioners. Furthermore, the PRI detail for us what ESG integration *does not* entail, including: prohibiting investment in certain sectors, countries, or companies; ignoring traditional risk factors, like interest risk; analysing *every* ESG issue affecting a company/issuer; having every investment decision affected by ESG issues; making *major* changes to one's investment processes; and sacrificing returns for one's portfolio.[32] We can see here the concept of potentially kowtowing to the world of finance in plain sight, which is why the PRI have been criticised. We shall look at these criticisms and constraints of the mainstreaming of ESG in the next subsection, but the argument that the integration of ESG into the investment process is still very much a 'subjective'[33] exercise is probably extremely difficult to argue against. Nevertheless, the PRI continue describing the practical application of the concept, and from different standpoints. For buy-side and sell-side brokers, ESG information is fed into their absolute valuation models. This means that both ESG and traditional financial factors affect their valuation of companies and helps to accurately adjust aspects such as future revenue growth rates, future operating costs, future capital expenditures, and so on. In fixed income, the focus on the creditworthiness of the issuer, which is all an investor will/should/does care about in reality. The PRI make the interesting observation that ESG integration helps an investor understand not only an entity's ability to repay outstanding debt, but in the case of countries especially, an entity's *willingness* to repay debt; sovereign debt is big business, and at the time of writing a number of poorer countries are struggling to service their debts on account of the COVID-19 pandemic and are faced with the tragic decision of either servicing their debt and preserving their access to the capital markets, or defaulting, subsequently becoming locked out of the capital markets, all to redirect the resources to their healthcare infrastructures.

There are also different forms that ESG integration can take. Wild notes how ESG integration can take a qualitative form whereby analysts consider ESG issues and factor those in, subjectively, to the in-depth analysis of a company's strengths and weaknesses. There is also a more quantitative form, where statistical data and rankings are injected into financial models. There are issues with this, as we shall see throughout the book, in terms of the reliability, timeliness, and nutritional value of ESG-related information, but the quantitative model is something that strongly interests analysts and is a main component of what they need from the process. As we saw earlier, the proliferation of AI and machine learning technologies are increasingly helping the all-important quantitative data component develop into a process which is genuinely helpful for investment strategies.

All of this development is geared towards one endpoint: to find what is *material*. Materiality is a key component for the mainstreaming of the concept, and rightly or wrongly is how everything is being framed so that as many conventional investors can turn the page. Surveys of the marketplace have been emphatic in declaring that materiality is the main concern of investors, and that ESG information will happily be factored in as long as it is relevant, and can potentially affect the reduction of risk.[34] Investors will likely take a twofold approach to considering what is material. First, they will examine a range of factors that may impact upon the issuer or investable opportunity, but may do this on a sector-specific base on the basis of efficiency and cost-efficiency. They will likely consider aspects that affect the rate of growth (via future revenue generation), associated costs, and any associated risks (perhaps through the governance of the company, etc.) It is usual that the three or four most impactful issues will be considered. Then, second, is the analysis of the associated timeframes. As Wild notes, 'it is important to clarify in which time frame these factors have the most significant impact'.[35] ESG issues usually play out over a longer time period than finance is usually accustomed to dealing with, mostly more than three years. We can see, therefore, that the longer the timeframe, the more subjective things become and, admittedly, the more riskier things become. Wild concludes by arguing that whilst the returns on this approach may not necessarily be better than, say, the 'best-in-class' approach, it does allow investors to claim the middle ground between concentrating on returns, but still focusing on sustainability. We shall see that, in the U.S. in particular, this divergence has been promoted as a key issue in the cultural, political, and legal senses.

Perhaps unsurprisingly however, the concept of 'materiality' is rooted in the development that Coffee described for us earlier. The attachment of the 'E' and the 'S' to the conventional 'G' is confirmed when we look at what investors consider to be the most material element from ESG as a broad concept. It should not be surprising that Governance has been consistently ranked as being, generally, of most importance for investors.[36] Furthermore, global surveys have revealed that 'globalisation and corporate governance' were amongst the most material for fund managers, although increasingly elements such as water usage and clean water, climate change, and environmental management were being actively considered alongside the 'G'. Additionally, Terrorism is playing a factor in deliberations.[37]

Materiality, then, is either the connecting philosophy that can change mainstream investing processes for the better, or an indication of the financing of ethical investment, which reduces the impact of the ethical investing cause. It is likely the case that without the blinkered focus on materiality, the investing arena would not be anywhere near where they currently are in terms of turning the corner away from the short-sighted return-focused position they were in even just a decade ago. However, the remarkable subjectivity that is not only being suggested, but *actively promoted* as an acceptable approach to turning this corner, does indeed raise questions as to how much 'finance' has actually changed. It has been noted in the literature that whilst the rate of ESG 'noise' in the marketplace is rapidly increasing, the rate of actual change in investment practice is negligible.[38] That may indeed be a generalism, but if we accept even the potential of it being true, then it is hardly surprising. What has been requested in not a slight alteration in investment practices, but a change in *culture*; the fear is that the market is paying lip-service to the ideal, but operating as usual. This leads to ask whether it is because of a reluctance to change, or the existence of too many hurdles in reality?

2.3 Constraints on a Concept

The mainstreaming of the concept of investing in a way that was not purely concerned with financial return was always going to be difficult. From the starting point, there have been problems both on the philosophical and practical sides of the equation. This was to be expected, but the question becomes how entrenched these problems are and, crucially, what can be done to resolve them. Some of the identified problems can be resolved with organisational alterations, but some are deep-rooted; for those problems, how does one change a culture when there is no leader or leadership structure in place? Even more so, can there be a leader, or a standard setter in such an environment?

Conventional economic and financial theory has been and continues to be dismissive of the concept of considering anything else other than financial metrics. One of the key concerns, which we know is particularly relevant to the mainstream financial arena as it is currently constituted, is that integrating ESG and considering any of the other approaches may harm diversification. Classical SRI naturally harms diversification by potentially excluding some investment opportunities from the range of options available. However, whilst it is rarely noted in the literature, can ESG integration said to be doing the same? It has been championed as the amalgamation of sustainable ideas and financial fundamentals, but would genuinely considering non-financial information impact upon the array of options available. What if, say, the 'S' concerns surrounding Saudi Arabia and its Human Rights record, its foreign wars, or repressive government indicated that investing in its flagship Aramco company was not an optimal option? What about the 'E'-based concerns regarding the company being one of the largest private CO2 producers on the planet? With the recent (partial) floating of this giant company, that conundrum was a real one. The result was that its shares surged on launching, and have continued to do well. We can infer that, when push comes to shove, financial opportunity will trump sustainability-related foresight. Perhaps the flexibility and subjectivity that seems to have been implanted within the mainstream-version of the concept allows for this, but the question becomes then what is the impact of the movement *really*?

Not only has this phenomenon been identified—Krosinsky argues that this incongruency is 'perhaps the most important battleground…'[39]—but it has been given an appropriate label. Butz and Laville have called it the 'materiality gap', and Robins explains that this means 'the tendency of SRI investors to address ESG issues only to the extent that they are financially material…'[40] One of the arguments that this phenomenon generates is that the mainstreaming of the concept means that the concept has lost its 'critical edge'. Robins, citing Hawken, discusses an uncomfortable reality for responsible investment champions in that 'striving to attain the highest rate of financial return is a direct cause of social injustice and environmental degradation as it consistently leads to externalisation of costs on the environment, the future, workers, and others'.[41] Similarly, Revelli tells us that 'for most funds the logic of SRI is, particularly in the context of ESG integration, to promote financial screening and then select companies considered to be most profitable and less risky from a financial point of view. Ethics is thus pushed into the background, resulting in the selection of the most virtuous companies among the best financially (not the most virtuous in the entire investment universe)'.[42] It is for this reason that modern-day 'responsible investment' has been heavily criticised for being incongruent; it has even been argued that funds and investors inappropriately, or even deceitfully, deploy whatever term is most appropriate for the marketplace (SRI, RI, ESG) and, upon inspection, their investment criteria does not replicate the sentiment. Similarly, it has even been suggested that some firms are merely 'providing a product which is in demand', which clearly indicates that the ethos of the movement is not being followed.[43] Other research has similarly found that investors are, to some extent, saying one thing and doing another,[44] which is precisely why initiatives like the PRI are being criticised for not doing more to enforce better behaviour.[45] There have been calls for asset managers to do much more,[46] but there could be an equally valid suggestion that *individual* investors should do more. Do those who hold pensions with pension funds really scrutinise their asset managers' approaches, and their adherence to what they signal they are doing? In reality, this is the consequence of dispersed ownership and an increasingly institutionalised landscape.

When all is said and done, individual investors want their returns (on investment, on their pension provision, or whatever investment they are holding), which allows for any potential incongruence to be witnessed.

On the topic of behaviour, it has been argued that 'behavioural impediments' are one of the largest hurdles to overcome, with an engrained scepticism being chief amongst the issues.[47] These impediments range from organisational scepticism, to a lack of belief in the ability to monetise the information, particularly over any sort of short-to-medium time horizon.[48] However, there are different takes on this behavioural obstruction, if it is true that it exists. Pinney et al. discuss a range of challenges facing the mainstreaming of the concept and describe an interesting challenge that could shed some light on the behavioural issues we have discussed. The scholars write that:

> While the last three years have seen significant progress in ESG integration, substantial challenges remain before we will be able to say that ESG is a fully integrated part of the US capital market system. The primary challenge continues to be the lack of a normative and widely accepted definition of ESG and standards for companies when measuring and reporting on ESG performance. A second challenge is the lack of understanding of and appreciation for ESG at the corporate governance level. Third is the size of the talent pool needed to support ESG integration, which is also formidable since it requires a combination of skills provided by few universities or colleges, including interdisciplinary knowledge and strategic policy experience along with deep investment expertise and the emotional intelligence skills to communicate with diverse corporate stakeholders. Finally, at least in the U.S., the organised pushback against ESG integration and shareholder activism around ESG by corporate and political interests remains a significant challenge.[49]

These identified challenges are particularly insightful. We have discussed the lack of a standard, but the second and third challenges are interconnected. The lack of appreciation and understanding of ESG, and what it can offer, comes from a lack of focused talent. This 'talent gap' has its roots in a number of different fields. Education has not anticipated this thematic change, and as such has not developed the talent pool to meet the demand; educational and certifying institutions are slowly catching up, but certainly not fast enough.[50] This potentially points at a systemic problem, as a recent survey found that of the 150 global institutional investors surveyed, 51% said that a lack of skills was the largest barrier they faced with regard to truly executing their ESG plans; 91% of respondents said that they expected to increase their ESG efforts over the next 5 years. With 78% of the respondents agreeing that having a good sustainability strategy improved returns, the problem is clear to see.[51] However, it is difficult to see a resolution in sight, because as Pinney et al. state, what is required is a talent base that can display a range of skills including interdisciplinary knowledge, strategic policy experience, deep investment expertise, and the 'emotional intelligence skills' to communicate all of this with diverse corporate stakeholders. It is not a surprise that there is a talent gap when those are the requirements. Perhaps, and I am just thinking out aloud here, the solution is to 'upskill' a number of people already within the institutions, and utilise their expertise and wide skill set. One would imagine attractive compensation packages would be needed for that to happen, and what this means more broadly is a genuine and deeper commitment by the firms themselves, i.e. time to put one's money where one's mouth is, perhaps. This is happening, to an extent, but it has created a new problem with the emergence of a 'talent war'; the scholars discuss how whilst leading firms such as the Big Three are constantly increasing their talent pools, there are not enough candidates truly capable of meeting the job specifications, which is leading to a competition for talent, which is 'particularly noticeable among top asset managers, and while there is no shortage of applicants, there are few that hold all the skills that such jobs require'.

If behaviour is an issue, and the lack of talent leading the movement from within can be attributed to that problem, then the last challenge the scholars identify is more worrying. The 'organised resistance' that the scholars describe, emanating from groups like the Chamber of Commerce and the Mainstream Investors Coalition (both in the U.S.), is a real obstacle for the movement. This is not just lobbying for lobbying's sakes, as the recent ruling by the Department of Labor—outlawing the consideration of non-financial information by institutional investors—clearly shows. We will be surveying the regulatory landscape in much greater detail later on in Chapters 4 and 5, but whilst it is likely that a Biden Administration will take some sort of action to lessen the effect of this development, the fact that it was allowed is a strong enough message for the sustainability movement; progression will certainly not come easy.

2.4 The Reality of an Ideal

The ideal of mainstreaming the concept of responsible finance, particularly after the Financial Crisis, is a necessary one. Whilst there have been crashes before, the aspiration to develop a better *culture* is admirable. After the Wall Street Crash of 1929 and the subsequent Great Depression, the focus was on mandating a cultural change (as seen with the focus turning to consumer protection via the Securities Acts of the 1930s). However, the approach for this era is one of encouraging cultural change from within. If such an aspiration turns out to be successful, the potential for developing a much more considered and forward-thinking system is real. However, as we have seen, there are a number of potential hurdles standing in the way of the realisation of that goal.

It may seem obvious, but before this movement took hold the concept of investing, and using anything other than purely financial metrics, was niche at best and widely dismissed at worst. It was the preserve of religiously-concerned investors, not mainstream institutional investors. In the wake of the Crisis, there was more than enough blame to go around and the investor base received their fair share. Whilst investment banks, credit rating agencies, and others received their fair share of blame, the question was asked as to why investors partook in the sub-prime market to the extent that they did. The answer, of course, was that they were chasing returns at any cost, without considering the underlying fundamentals. In many circumstances, they were relying on the credit rating agencies' estimations of creditworthiness, which for many reasons is particularly irresponsible. Moving forward, what was needed was a different approach, were those investors embody the concept of being *responsible*. Creating this atmosphere, theoretically, should lead to issuers of debt becoming more aware of their impact upon society, primarily through their need to access the capital that flows from the capital markets. In theory, it is all interlinked.

However, what the idealists have found is that the financial arena has its own rules, and they are *engrained*. They are engrained not out of choice, but more out of a systemic adherence to a principle; the system is concerned with making money. The clue is in the name of capitalism. What the idealists wanted is for capitalists to pause, and then to consider if their actions were aligned to a broader humanist objective. What they found, predictably, is that this was not the case. Yet, it is far too tempting to assign this to capitalistic greed. In reality, the system is a system of competing pressures, which all take their toll. For example, we saw that corporations *do* understand that considering ESG in their processes is beneficial; but, in reality, they do not have the expertise to fully lead on this movement. To that end, the educational infrastructure that supports the financial arena has not provided the market with the expertise it needs, but it is catching up. The 'upskilling' of people who have the necessary experience is underway, but not taking shape fast enough for the market. In another example, there have been concerns raised regarding the legality of managers in fiduciary roles taking action on behalf of their principal; to get around that problem (which has just crystallised in the U.S.), lawyers have promoted the concept of *integrating* ESG into a much larger financially-concerned apparatus, and even then only when it is considered financially *material*.

The concept of materiality has been the concept that has both driven the movement forward, and for the traditionalists what is also holding it back. For financial market participants, the concept of materiality allows them to include themselves within this ever-growing marketplace and, crucially, signal to the market, their own investor base, and anybody else (like regulators) that they are being 'responsible'. However, critics argue fervently that this is not what responsible investing should be; it is not for ethics to be forced to conform for finance, but for finance to be forced to conform for ethics. In reality, the latter is simply not happening. The question is why? The infrastructure around finance that lends to it authority, namely onlookers and academe, mainly paint the picture of 'how material is ESG?', which in itself frames the issue from a particularly biased angle. However, one may argue that this is what they really should be doing because, quite simply, this is reality and, in reality, there is a need for change. Change, even if incrementally witnessed, is still change. To that end, the scope of the buy-in, on the surface at least, to this movement, is truly remarkable. There is no one definitive statistic, but it is not inappropriate to say that trillions of dollars in Assets under Management (AuM) have bought into this movement. Surely that is positive?

It is not for me to tell you, the reader, what the answer is to that question. But, what is worth knowing are the constraints to the movement and, more importantly, understanding clearly what we are trying to learn. The focus of this book is on learning more about what I am calling the 'battle for the mainstream' between the sustainability rating agencies, and the credit rating agencies. In this chapter, we have been exposed to the 'mainstream' and we now know that it has particular characteristics.

In displaying the developments of society over the past few decades, we now are faced with a highly institutionalised financial arena. Whilst the rates of institutionalisation may differ between jurisdiction (the U.S. is more institutionalised than the E.U., for example), the pattern is a clear one. Institutionalised investors require different things from that of the traditional retail investor, and this difference is only heightened when we consider that there is almost an oligopoly in the institutionalised arena between the Big Three of BlackRock, State Street, and Vanguard. So, what does the 'mainstream' actually want? Well, because a lot of them are what are known as 'universal investors', they are more inclined to take a longer view than a 'normal' investor. This means they are somewhat inclined to a. buy into the movement more, and b. take concerted action to move that movement forward. However, they need the talent in order to do it, and are more than willing to participate in competition to get it because of its scarcity. They also need the information to take action. Large institutional investors have the resources to develop their own ESG-based information, and they do so systematically. They do not have the access to the issuers that a third-party organisation can gain because of the independence that comes with being a third party. Even if that third party is being paid by that issuer to develop the information, the independence outweighs the potential conflict of interest, and for one specific reason: the third-party allows the investor to *signal* a number of things to a number of parties. The investor, in utilising the information of a third-party organisation(s), can *signal* to their principal that they are taking particular actions, can *signal* to regulators that they are taking particular actions, and can *signal* to the marketplace that they are taking particular actions. All of this has the potential of transforming the marketplace. Yet, there are problems with this.

The information that is needed is either not forthcoming, or massively stunted when it does. Investors are routinely complaining that information from ESG providers is too slow to be received, lacking value, and most importantly cannot be compared easily enough. Such large investors live off the assimilation of information within their processes, and a poor supply line for that information can have massive consequences. Because of that, it is understandable that firms are currently in the 'lip-service' stage of the movement; it is too dangerous to not get involved, but the infrastructure is not strong enough to fully commit. If we move past the philosophical debate regarding what 'responsible finance' *should* be for a moment, then what the mainstream needs from its data providers is clear: comparability, reliability, and timeliness. The question is whether the current ESG informational arena can meet that demand. To find out whether it can or not, and what the consequences may be of it not being able to meet the demand of the mainstream, we shall now meet the sustainability rating agencies and learn more about their industry. After that, we will meet the credit rating agencies and understand their industry more too. With this chapter in mind, we will see that the *battle* is already underway and that, eventually, the mainstream will get what it needs. The question is what form will that provision take?

Notes

1. Cary Krosinsky and Nick Robins, *Sustainable Investing: The Art of Long-Term Performance* (Earthscan 2008) xxi.
2. Enrique Ballestero, Blanca Perez-Gladish, and Ana Garcia-Bernabeu, 'The Ethical Financial Question and the MCDM Framework' in Enrique Ballestero, Blanca Perez-Gladish, and Ana Garcia-Bernabeu, *Socially Responsible Investment: A Multi-Criteria Decision Making Approach* (Springer 2014) 5.
3. Tessa Hebb, 'Introduction – The Next Generation of Responsible Investing' in Tessa Hebb, *The Next Generation of Responsible Investing* (Springer 2011) 1.
4. John Cullis, Philip Jones, and Alan Lewis, 'Ethical Investing: Where are we Now?' in Morris Altman, *Handbook of Contemporary Behavioural Economics: Foundations and Developments* (Routledge 2015) 605.
5. Ibid.
6. Sakis Kotsantonis, Chris Pinney, and George Sarafeim, 'ESG Integration in Investment Management: Myths and Realities' (2016) 28 *Journal of Applied Corporate Finance* 2 12.
7. Kate Miles, *The Origins of International Investment Law: Empire, Environment and the Safeguarding of Capital* (Cambridge University Press 2013) 240.
8. Nick Robins, 'The Emergence of Sustainable Investing' in Cary Krosinsky, *Sustainable Investing: The Art of Long-Term Performance* (Earthscan 2012) 12.
9. John C. Coffee, 'The Future of Disclosure: ESG, Common Ownership, and Systemic Risk' (2020) European Corporate Governance Institute: Law Working Paper No. 541/2020. https://scholarship.law.columbia.edu/cgi/viewcontent.cgi?article=3684&context=faculty_scholarship. 2.
10. (n 2) 8.
11. Murat Çizakça, *Islamic Capitalism and Finance: Origins, Evolution and the Future* (Edward Elgar 2011) xx.

12. (n 2) 8.
13. (n 11).
14. Olaf Weber, 'Finance and Sustainability' in Harald Heinrichs, Pim Martens, Gerd Michelsen, and Arnim Wiek, *Sustainability Science: An Introduction* (Springer 2015) 121.
15. Ibid.
16. (n 3) 1.
17. Christophe Revelli, 'Socially Responsible Investing (SRI): From Mainstream to Margin?' [2017] 39 *Research in International Business and Finance* 711–717, 712.
18. Cary Krosinsky and Sophie Purdom, 'Introduction: The Future of Investing Is Sustainable' in Cary Krosinsky and Sophie Purdom, *Sustainable Investing: Revolutions in Theory and Practice* (Taylor & Francis 2016) 7.
19. Schroders, *Understanding Sustainable Investment and ESG Investment Terms* (2017). http://www.schroders.com/getfunddocument?oid=1.9.2760595, 7.
20. (n 9) 24.
21. Christophe Revelli, 'Socially Responsible Investment (SRI): Meta-Debate and Development Perspectives' in Bernard Paranque and Roland Perez, *Finance Reconsidered: New Perspectives for a Responsible and Sustainable Finance* (Emerald 2016) 161.
22. David A. Lubin and Daniel C. Esty 'The Sustainability Imperative' in Cary Krosinsky, Nick Robins, and Stephen Viederman *Evolutions in Sustainable Investing: Strategies, Funds and Thought Leadership* (Wiley 2014) 2.
23. Siobhan Riding, 'ESG Funds Forecast to Outnumber Conventional Funds by 2025' (2020) *Financial Times* (Oct 17). https://www.ft.com/content/5cd6e923-81e0-4557-8cff-a02fb5e01d42.
24. Chris Pinney, Sophie Lawrence, and Stephanie Lau, 'Sustainability and Capital Markets – Are We There Yet?' (2019) 31 *Journal of Applied Corporate Finance* 2 86–91, 86.
25. Valeria Venturelli, Alessia Pedrazzoli, and Elisabetta Gualandri, 'From Seeker Side to Investor Side: Gender Dynamics in UK Equity Crowdfunding Investments' in Elisabette Gualandri, Valeria Venturelli, and Alex Sclip, *Frontier Topics in Banking: Investigating New Trends and Recent Development in the Financial Industry* (Springer 2019) 101.
26. (n 17) 714.
27. Ibid., 713.
28. Sakis Kotsantonis, Chris Pinney, and George Sarafeim, 'ESG Integration in Investment Management: Myths and Realities' (2016) 28 *Journal of Applied Corporate Finance* 2 10–96.
29. (n 3) 4.

30. Hager Jemel-Fornetty, Celine Louche, and David Bourghelle, 'Changing the Dominant Convention: The Role of Emerging Initiatives in Mainstreaming ESG' in William Sun, Celine Louche, and Roland Perez, *Finance and Sustainability: Towards a New Paradigm? A Post-Crisis Agenda* (Emerald 2011) 87.
31. (n 21) 159.
32. PRI, *ESG in Equity Analysis and Credit Analysis: An Overview* (PRI, 2018). https://www.unpri.org/download?ac=4571.
33. Barry B. Burr, 'ESG Integration on Rise, But Issues Remain: Agreement Needed on Weighting, Scoring, and Definitions, Still It's Moving Toward Mainstream' (2016) 44 *Pensions & Investments* 7.
34. Keyur Patel, 'ESG Investing Moves to the Mainstream' (2018) 74 *Financial Analysts Journal* 3 39–41, 40.
35. Daniel Wild, 'ESG Integration Approach' in Swiss Sustainable Finance, *Handbook on Sustainable Investments: Background Information and Practical Examples for Institutional Asset Owners* (CFA Institute Research Foundation 2017) 55–57.
36. OECD, *OECD Business and Finance Outlook 2020 Sustainable and Resilient Finance* (OECD Publishing 2020) 98.
37. Jill Solomon, *Corporate Governance and Accountability* (Wiley 2020) 237.
38. Diana-Michaela Ţîrcă, Anişoara-Niculina Apetri, and Mirela I. Aceleanu, 'Sustainability in Finance and Economics' in Magdalena Ziolo and Bruno S. Sergi, *Financing Sustainable Development: Key Challenges and Prospects* (Springer 2019) 10.
39. Cary Krosinsky, 'Sustainable Equity Investing: The Market-Beating Strategy' in Cary Krosinsky, *Sustainable Investing: The Art of Long-Term Performance* (Earthscan 2012) 19.
40. (n 8) 15.
41. Ibid.
42. (n 17) 715.
43. William Ransome and Charles Sampford, *Ethics and Socially Responsible Investment: A Philosophical Approach* (Ashgate Publishing 2013) 50.
44. (n 38).
45. (n 28) 12.
46. Attracta Mooney, 'Companies Defy Investor Demands on Climate Change' (2020) *Financial Times* (Nov 8). https://www.ft.com/content/798f752a-5db1-498c-8d1d-6389b66f317d.
47. (n 30) 88.
48. Benjamin J. Richardson, *Fiduciary Law and Responsible Investing: In Nature's Trust* (Routledge 2013) 4.
49. (n 24) 86.
50. Claudia Kruse and Michael Schmidt, 'Sustainable Governance and Leadership' in Paul G. Fisher, *Making the Financial System Sustainable* (Cambridge University Press 2020) 148.

51. Zak Bentley, 'Macquarie Survey Shows Skills Shortage Holding Back Investors' ESG Efforts' (2020) Infrastructure Investor (Jan 17). https://www.infrastructureinvestor.com/macquarie-survey-shows-skills-shortage-holding-back-investors-esg-efforts/.

CHAPTER 3

The Sustainability Rating Industry

So, the mainstream is developing at a quite a pace. But it is also clear that its development so far has been one in spirit only, and even that has been questioned. It is only in spirit only because, only up until recently,' the informational infrastructure needed to facilitate the genuine incorporation of ethical/CSR (Corporate Social Responsibility)/ESG principles was sorely lacking. The Financial Crisis inspired a new debate on what could be a more sustainable future, but 'the existing tools, frameworks and mechanisms to measure corporate sustainability are not adequate'.[1] The marketplace, as it is designed to do, is now seeking ways to fill that void and morph the solution into exactly the form that *it* needs.

In the last chapter, we spoke about how there are competing forces at play and how those forces are attempting to enforce their will on the development of the 'movement'. In this chapter, we shall see how that is currently playing out in one particular field, as the so-called sustainability rating industry is being scrutinised like never before; the scrutiny is focusing upon whether the industry is 'fit for purpose'. We are now starting to see just what that purpose is and that, with regard to the need of the 'mainstream', the purpose is very particular. The mainstream investor base is a static factor in this sense, i.e. it will have its needs met, either way. It is not the static investor base who will change their approach to suit the rating industries; the focus is on *serving* the investor base, not the other way around.

D. Cash, *Sustainability Rating Agencies vs Credit Rating Agencies*, Palgrave Studies in Impact Finance,
https://doi.org/10.1007/978-3-030-71693-6_3

Because of that, we need to know the sustainability rating agencies inside and out. In this chapter, we will do that. However, there is something that needs to be discussed immediately, and we will cover this in much more detail in the next section. The credit rating industry and its associated terminologies are cemented, and consistent. The 'Big Three'—S&P Global, Moody's, and Fitch Ratings—are *credit rating agencies*. They dominate a market that has few large players, and their product is distinct from associated industries like the *credit reference agencies*—like Dun & Bradstreet—who whilst they share a lineage, are clearly distinct. Yet, in the 'sustainable rating agency' industry, that is definitely not the case. In fact, there is not even a recognised moniker for the industry itself! I use the terminology of 'sustainable rating agency' here because it has been used before and also, to my mind, it denotes the concept of rating entities with regards to their focus on sustainability. However, that is certainly not universal, and nor is the constitution of the industry itself. Some of the major players do not provide rankings or ratings, but are index developers—so why are they called agencies? Some only look at certain factors like the consideration of climate change effects, etc., whilst many have different information gathering approaches and remuneration models. The young age of the 'industry', together with the vast access to technology and information (something that was massively lacking during the formation of the credit rating industry as we shall see in the next chapter), has led to a marketplace filled with a variety of different actors. As we shall now see, this is problematic for the mainstream investor base. Although I am foreshadowing analyses that we will undertake shortly, it needs to be declared that, from this point on, I will be referring to the participants in this industry as 'CSSs' which stands for *Corporate Sustainability Systems*. This terminology was developed by Diez-Cañamero et al. and I believe that it is the most suitable for what we are focusing on. This is because, as the authors state:

> The financial market is pushing the development of Socially Responsible Investment, which has led to the rise of Corporate Sustainability Systems. These CSSs are tools that rate corporate performance on sustainability. However, they constitute a chaotic universe, with instruments of different nature. This paper identifies and groups the common characteristics of the CSSs into three different typologies: Indexes, Rankings, and Ratings.[2]

It is so important for the future of the CSS industry that this 'chaotic universe' is simplified because the simplification of complex understandings, data, and concepts is of crucial importance to the mainstream. This is because the mainstream, as we shall see in Chapter 4, need to *signal* to the uninterested and the uninitiated, and diverse data providers to do not allow for that fundamental need to be met. Therefore, let us meet the CSSs and their chaotic universe, in the hope of understanding it more.

3.1 The Development of the Corporate Sustainability System Industry: A 'Chaotic Universe'

A large number of the CSSs we shall meet shortly started years before the Financial Crisis took shape. However, their relevance is only recently growing. The mainstream market now requires sustainability-related information to be fed into their processes, in order to invest as responsibly as they can whilst still garnering the level of returns they need. This is quite a requirement. This is why it has been said that 'the responsibility of ESG rating agencies cross financial market boundaries since the consequences of dynamic changes in corporate sustainability assessments by ESG rating agencies go beyond the scope of financial markets, affecting the society as a whole'.[3] It goes beyond the scope of financial markets because not only are the world's largest investors taking the lead (so it is argued by many) in the movement to a more sustainable future, but the act of rating an entity has the potential to shape that entity's development, trajectory, and internal policies. It has been found that financial entities will tend to focus more on their sustainability-related practices when in need of maintaining, or increasing their reputation in the markets.[4] This may be acceptable, but when it has also been found that many CSSs operate a 'tick box' approach,[5] it calls into question the sincerity of that sustainability-related development. Nevertheless, the role of the CSS is not just in declaring a view. In this nascent market, they have the potential of being market-makers. Furthermore, they have a key role in defining the direction of the sustainability movement for the mainstream—that may sound like an exaggeration, but we shall see in this book that the role of the third-party verifier with regard to 'ratings' is a key component to the health of a movement, whether it be for financial or sustainable ends.

Before we meet the CSSs, it is worth understanding on a very basic level what it is they do. There are, naturally, different takes on this. Pagano et al. describe for us the concept of a duality of need, based upon the 'demand by investors to better evaluate their portfolio companies' ESG performance', against 'a growing number of companies [that] are seeking external ESG metric to measure and validate their ESG efforts, with some even linking pay to these metrics'.[6] On the part of the investor base, the authors give is a simple understanding upon which we can build when they declare that 'every investment needs a benchmark'. This is helpful, and they continue by illustrating that 'in a competitive market economy, all economic actors are constantly calibrating their performance in relative and absolute terms against their peers'. For the issuing entities, the CSSs and their outputs can be considered as 'opinions and assessments about how well a company manages to balance ESG issues. It measures companies' ability to benefit from opportunities and manage risks in the mid- to long-term'.[7] The CSSs essentially 'seek to make corporations' environmental [and social and governance] effects more transparent'.[8] This aim at increasing the levels of transparency within the arena is both where the CSSs find their cause, and their greatest threat. We shall see at the end of this chapter and throughout the book that there are *many* criticisms of the CSSs with regard to their own transparency, but they do indeed have a particularly important role when it comes to the flow of information. They serve to reduce the 'informational asymmetry' that exists within the financial arena, and in this particular sector. Informational asymmetry describes the process whereby there is a 'gap' in the knowledge needed by one party, and that can be provided by the other. It is too costly for investors to undertake the assessment of every investable opportunity, and the duplicative costs would create inefficiencies at the level which would make investing unattractive, if not unprofitable. For the issuers, there would be a duplication of requests for information from them, and then that information may itself be commercially sensitive. Therefore, within that void, there exist third-parties (fewer than the investor base, of course) that can liaise with the issuers and alter the communication of that may be commercially sensitive, but in a way that it still conveys the relevance of the information, i.e. through ratings and rankings. For investors, the CSSs provide necessary information for a fraction of the price that it would cost the investor to find, and also the presence of a seemingly independent third party allows for the investor to meet the requirements set by their principals, and regulators etc. The

CSSs are, on paper, serving a *systemic* need that is inherent within the financial marketplace—just like auditors do when verifying the accounts and practices of financial entities, etc.

With that systemic role understood, it is not surprising that the focus by the mainstream on sustainability since the Financial Crisis has become the seedbed for an explosion of growth in the CSS industry. The UN Global Compact, a non-binding initiative aimed at encouraging companies to focus more on their sustainability (formed in 2000) has been identified as a starting point for this growth.[9] Since then, there has been an array of formations, mergers and acquisitions (M&A), and industry movements. Pagano et al. note that 'the total size of the market for ESG ratings and ESG indexes... is difficult to precisely measure'. They identify how it took just ten years from 2000 to 2010 for the parties within the CSS universe to jump from 21 to 108, and that rate has increased since. A 2013 report identified over 250 providers around the world, whilst others have suggested there are around 200. A good example of the complexity on offer, even when trying to understand who is in the 'chaotic universe', can be seen with the understanding that MSCI (who we will meet shortly) operate over 700 ESG equity and fixed income indices.[10]

Furthermore, the expansion of the marketplace has been profound and led to some of the world's largest financial service providers taking a great interest in the industry. For example, as Berg et al. describe:

> ESG ratings first emerged in the 1980s as a service for investors to screen companies not purely on financial characteristics, but also on characteristics relating to social and environmental performance. The earliest ESG rating agency Vigeo-Eiris was established in 1983 in France and five years later Kinder, Lydenberg & Domini (KLD) was established in the US. While initially catering to a highly-specialised investor clientele, such as faith-based organisations, the market for ESG ratings has widened dramatically, especially in the past decade. Estimates are that 30 trillion USD are invested in ways that rely on some form of ESG information, a figure that has grown by 34 percent since 2016. As interest in sustainable investing grew, many early providers were acquired by established financial data providers, e.g. MSCI bought KLD in 2010, Morningstar bought Sustainalytics in 2010, ISS bought Oekom in 2018, and Moody's bought Vigeo-Eiris in 2019.[11]

The amount of change in the CSS universe is difficult to keep up with, and there are different ways of understanding the market, unfortunately; the concept of there being 'misaligned narratives'[12] between market participants and academics is certainly appropriate in this sense, amongst others. A good example of this is with the excellent work conducted by Diez-Cañamero et al. utilising the work of SustainAbility, via their *Rate the Raters Report* in 2019. This is an accepted standard for understanding the marketplace, yet it is incomplete. In a previous work, I have attempted to update their understanding to make it as holistic and accurate as possible, and I will again do this to bring the understanding as up-to-date as is possible.[13]

The *Rate the Raters* report clarifies that there are 11 entities that they consider as 'agencies'. This is why the usage of the term CSSs is more appropriate, because that list of 11 includes entities such as Bloomberg and ISS, who only offer scores and ratings as a product in a line of many. Also, there are some entities missing from the list that should be included, and even since 2019 there has been a slew of M&A activity. So, for the purposes of understanding the market in its entirety, we shall go through each CSS in turn.

3.1.1 CDP Climate, Water, and Forest Scores

The Carbon Disclosure Project, founded in 2002, has developed into a global non-profit organisation comprising of several initiatives. One such initiative is its Climate, Water, and Forest Scores. We will focus more on the methodology employed by CDP in a later section, but in essence it seeks to score companies and cities on themes related to climate change, water resources and scarcity, and the impact upon forests. So far, the initiative provides scores for more than 8000 companies and nearly 1000 countries, and their methodological processes are particularly extensive. Aspects considered range from the entity's focus on reducing carbon emissions, to their supply chain's effect upon deforestation, etc. Their rating scale runs from A to F, and this scale also contains modifiers (like + and -). As I noted in the previous work, it is interesting that respondents to the Rate the Raters Report noted that they found the CDP scores as the most 'useful' across the array of options, although it was also noted by Shahzad et al. that CDP only use data that is voluntarily reported, so the potential for bias to influence the scoring is acute.[14]

3.1.2 *RobecoSAM*

RobecoSAM is consistently referred to in commentators' lists of CSSs but, since 2019 it technically no longer exists. The company started as two separate entities—SAM (Sustainable Asset Management) was started in 1995, but was taken over by the much more established Robeco in 2006 (Robeco was founded in 1929). The company was known around the world for its Corporate Sustainability Assessment, which involved inviting nearly 2500 of the world's largest companies to participate in being assessed. The process would consist of questionnaires ranging from between 80 and 120 questions, and the answers would be prescribed a score which would feed into the 'Total Sustainability Score'. The process would involve cross-checking the answers with publicly-available information, and the services of Deloitte as a third-party verifier. However, in 2019 the credit rating giant S&P Global purchases SAM, and incorporated its talent base and processes into its new 'S&P Global ESG Scores' product launched in May 2020. The SAM brand has been retained, and Robeco has access to its analysis via the deal. The CSA has been retained, although it has been rebranded as the 'SAM Sustainability Yearbook' and consists of the same processes.

3.1.3 *Sustainalytics*

Sustainalytics is a brand that is very well known in the ESG rating arena, and in 2020 the credit rating outsider Morningstar acquired the company in full. The company started as an amalgamation of 4 companies in 2009 and a year later they launched their Country ESG Risk Research & Ratings service which sat aside their corporate ratings service. We will look at the rating methodology in more detail shortly when we look at a few CSS profiles in increased detail, but their scale runs from 1 to 100. They look at up to 70 indictors for each industry, and then the assessments are divided up between preparedness, disclosure, and performance. The company then liaises with the company in question to obtain more relevant information, if appropriate.

3.1.4 *MSCI ESG Ratings*

MSCI is a major financial entity, standing for Morgan Stanley Capital International. Their *ESG Ratings* service sits within their much larger company and was launched in 2010. Its rating scale runs from AAA to CCC, and despite sitting within a larger company the service is one of the most extensive in the marketplace, covering more than 6000 companies and more than 400,000 equity and fixed-income securities. The service focuses upon 37 key ESG-related issues, with the dominant themes being climate change, natural resources, pollution and waste, environmental opportunities, human capital, product liability, stakeholder opposition, social opportunities, corporate governance, and corporate behaviour. The service collects its information via a range of sources, including governmental databases, company disclosures, and academic and NGO databases. Like Sustainalytics, the service offers the chance for target companies to inform the process before the publication of the score.

3.1.5 Bloomberg (ESG Scores)

Whilst the MSCI offering may be the most extensive offering in the marketplace, the offering from Bloomberg is certainly the most widely available offering. This is because their ESG scores sit within their Bloomberg 'terminals', which is a piece of software that allows users access to the universe of market data provided by Bloomberg, and also allow it to place trades, etc. This means that at least some data is held on over 100,000 companies. The system utilises information from a range of resources, including company sustainability reports, annual reports, websites, and conversations with companies themselves. Their processes consider more than 120 ESG factors.

3.1.6 ISS-Oekom

ISS-Oekom's offering is a great example of the changes that occur within the industry. Oekom Research AG was a German company founded in 1993. In March 2018, the proxy-voting service ISS (Institutional Shareholder Services) purchased Oekom Research AG. In demonstrating the changes, ISS itself was once owned by MSCI but was sold to Genstar Capital in 2014. After incorporating and maintaining the brand, the brand was altered and it now is referred to as ISS ESG. ISS used to consider a number of 'G'overnance-related issues via its 'ISS QualityScore', but with the acquisition of Oekom Research the QualityScore has just been expanded to create the 'Governance QualityScore' that contains research on over 6000 companies. The service provides ratings and rankings on a number of different elements including corporates, countries, sustainability bonds, and more. The CSS utilises publicly available information, as well as dialogue with the target companies (via a variety of methods).

3.1.7 FTSE Russell ESG Ratings

FTSE Russell is a data provision service of the FTSE International Limited company (FTSE standing for Financial Times Stock Exchange). The company's history is related to the developments of the FTSE group between Pearson (the former parent of the Financial Times), and now the London Stock Exchange Group (LSE), who wholly own the service. As we shall see shortly, the LSE are close to taking a massive stake in the CSS arena. Nevertheless, whilst the main group operates more than 250,000 indices, the FTSE Russell service provides ESG-related data on more than 7000 securities, utilising more than 300 indicators to categorise such research.

3.1.8 EcoVadis

EcoVadis, formed in Paris in 2007, is rather unique in the leading CSS universe in that it has a distinct specialism. It focuses upon the supply chain and providing sustainability-related information for procurement teams. It says that it is the 'most trusted provider of business sustainability ratings, intelligence and collaborative performance improvement tools for global supply chains'. It carries rating on more than 60,000 entities, and its methodology is founded upon seven distinct principles. Ratings must be: evidence based; the industry sector, country, and size *matter*; there must be a diversification of courses; technology is a must; the ratings must be conducted by internationally-leading CSR experts; there is always to be traceability and transparency; and finally everything is pinned to the mentality that one can achieve excellence via continuous improvement. The company utilises publicly available information, information from the rated company themselves, and then third-party endorsements. The company is developing and this is witnessed in the recent investments from powerhouses such as CVC (who invested $200 million in January 2020), and Bain & Co.

3.1.9 Thomson Reuters ESG Scores

In demonstrating how quickly the market can change from the Rate the Raters report in 2019, the offering from Thomson Reuters is a clear example of an ever-changing industry. Thomson Reuters, the Canadian-based media conglomerate, purchased a data provider called Asset4 in 2009 and, in 2015, used this collaboration to create the Thomson Reuters ESG Scores. With Thomson Reuters' backing, the Scores became a major component of the industry. In 2018, *Refinitiv* was created as a joint venture between Thomson Reuters and BlackRock, with a large proportion of the ESG scores service being transferred to the new entity. This transfer came at the cost of around $20 billion, but today the London Stock Exchange is just awaiting regulatory approval from European Antitrust authorities for their $27 billion acquisition of *Refinitiv*. The service offered contains data on more than 5000 public companies across the world. It contains more than 200 indicators which are applied, and then scores are weighted against a number of categories ranging from industry and sector variables.

3.1.10 Vigeo-Eiris

Identified as one of the early runners in the industry, it is actually the EIRIS element of the firm that contains the traditional element. EIRIS, founded in 1983 (standing for Ethical Investment Research Services) was a Charity founded by a group of religiously-focused British ethical investors (such as Churches etc.), to aid Churches to incorporate ethical perspectives into their investment practices. It partnered with FTSE to found the FTSE4Dood initiative in 2001. Meanwhile, Vigeo, after acquiring a number of smaller European players, merged with EIRIS in 2015 to become Vigeo-Eiris. The partnership as an entity would only last for 4 years, because in 2019 the credit rating giant Moody's purchased the outfit to further develop its ESG offerings. Moody's in fact soon withdrew its Green Bond assessment service, instead moving the responsibility to its newly acquired unit.

The service and its methodology are very compartmentalised. There are 38 sustainability criteria that are then split over six domains; these are then segmented into more than 40 sub-frameworks, which are then run through more than 300 indicators. The six domains include environment, community involvement, business behaviour, human rights, governance, and human resources.

3.1.11 Standard Ethics

Standard Ethics is not included in the Rate the Raters report, but I include it in this list. The agency has grown steadily since being established in 2001. It utilises the issuer-pays model utilises more widely in the credit rating industry, but the agency tries to declare its independence by stating that it does not provide ancillary services in addition to its rating products—this has been identified as being a key facilitator of conflicts of interests within the credit rating industry.[15] This remuneration model influences its methodologies, as there is no questionnaire that the majority of other agencies use. The fact that their ratings are solicited by paying issuers means that their methodology is analyst-driven. The agency adopts a E- to EEE rating scale. Whilst the agency states that it does not use weightings like its competitors, but rather a unique algorithm, looking closer at the said algorithm reveals that weights are factored in; the basic weightings applied are governance at 33%, stakeholders at 18%, transparency at 14%, market and position at 13%, and environment at 8%.

Whilst the methodological variances are clear to see from the profiles above, the actual approach may not be so clear from the descriptions included. In order to provide more information, a profile of some of the main players in the list above can be useful to further understand how these CSSs actually come to the rating that they do. It will also provide fantastic context for the analysis that will follow, namely the myriad of criticisms that are now being levelled at the CSS universe, particularly regarding their methodologies.

3.2 Methodologies in Focus

Information on the CSSs' methodologies is more available for some rather than others. This is sometimes because a CSS may sit within a much larger organisation, or presents itself as offering a rating product amongst a range of other services. Also, the lack of regulation for the industry—which we will discuss later on—reveals itself here as unlike in the credit rating industry, where the agencies must publish their methodological underpinnings in order to be registered with the relevant authorities. However, there is useful information available. In this section, the focus will be on the methodologies of Sustainalytics and MSCI ESG Scores. The reason that these CSSs have been chosen is because they are, perhaps, the most forthcoming with details regarding their methodologies. Only CDP perhaps compares, but their questionnaire-based approach is particularly extensive and very relative to the user in question.[16]

3.2.1 Sustainalytics

Sustainalytics make clear that their ESG Risk Ratings measure the 'degree to which a company's economic value is at risk driven by ESG factors or, more technically speaking, the magnitude of a company's unmanaged ESG risks. A company's ESG Risk Rating is comprised of a quantitative score and a risk category'.[17] This sentiment neatly aligns with the sentiment of the 'mainstreamisation' of the sustainable mission; the focus on the protection of the economic value of the company is a key determinant for the movement. The agency confirms this further when they declare for users that:

> An issue is considered to be material within the ESG Risk Ratings if its presence or absence in financial reporting is likely to influence the decisions made by a reasonable investor. To be considered relevant in the ESG Risk Ratings, an issue must have a potentially substantial impact on the economic value of a company and, hence, its financial risk – and return profile from an investment perspective.

As we shall see in the next section, comparability is a key issue affecting this industry. In attempting to combat that issue, Sustainalytics have developed an approach that consists of grouping a company, based on their quantitative scoring, into one of five risk categories—negligible, low, medium, high, and severe. This has the effect, according to Sustainalytics, of allowing one to compare say, a bank, to an entity like an oil refinery company. The agency is seemingly proud of this, declaring that 'with the ESG Risk Ratings' scores, we have introduced a single currency for ESG risk'. Yet, the important question is how do they make seemingly unconnected industries, each of which is affected by very different ESG factors, comparable?

They do this by building a rating upon three particular building blocks: Corporate Governance; Material ESG Issues; and Idiosyncratic ESG Issues. Corporate Governance is identified by the agency as being perhaps the foundational element to their ratings, mainly because the act of doing so 'reflects [the agency's] conviction that poor Corporate Governance poses material risks for companies. It applies to all companies in our rating universe, irrespective of the subindustry they are in'.[18] Whilst the agency states that Corporate Governance-related risk may affect companies in different ways depending upon Industry or location etc., they believe that Corporate Governance risks contribute about 20% on average to the overall unmanaged risk score.

Material ESG issues occur at the subindustry level for Sustainalytics, and they are reviewed annually. They refer to a set of topics or issues that require management initiatives or similar levels of oversight. Cited examples for just one element—the material issue of Human Capital—include employee recruitment, development, diversity, and labour relations. In a somewhat contradictory manner perhaps, the agency declares that the Material ESG Issues block forms the core and centre of their methodology, only a paragraph or two after declaring that Corporate Governance is a foundational element; perhaps they see all three as having equal importance. Nevertheless, whilst declaring that Material ESG Issues can impact almost any company but in a fairly predictable manner, there are some issues that are less predictable and the agency labels these as 'Idiosyncratic ESG Issues'. These issues are unpredictable and unexpected in the sense that they do not necessarily relate to the target industry or subindustry. The cited example is an accounting scandal, that cannot necessarily be expected to affect a certain industry over another.

Differentiating between these two versions of ESG risks and their predictability is useful, but it is not the full story. For instance, and particularly in relation to the material predictable ESG issues, what effect should it have whether a risk can be fully managed or not? Sustainalytics apply a 'manageable risk factor' (MRF) for this purpose and predefine this at the subindustry level. These MRFs range from 30 to 100%, and essentially represent the exposure to a particular material ESG issue that should be, at least theoretically, manageable by the company. There are four primary factors considered when developing an MRF. The ability of the company to ensure compliance by its employees via health and safety regulations, for example, is considered. The effects of outside actors on the ability of the management to manage the issue (i.e. cybersecurity), the complexity of the particular issue (i.e. global supply chains), and also the physical limitations on innovations or technological factors are also considered. This focus on management is an important part of the agency's assessments, as:

> The ESG Risk Ratings' second dimension is Management. It can be considered as a set of company commitments, actions and outcomes that demonstrate how well a company is managing the ESG risks it is exposed to.
>
> The overall management score for a company is derived from a set of management indicators (policies, management systems, certifications, etc.) and outcome-focused indicators. Outcome-focused indicators measure management performance either directly in quantitative terms (e.g. CO2 emissions or CO2 intensity) or via a company's involvement in controversies (represented by a company's event indicators).[19]

In order to allow for as thorough an assessment as they can, the agency reviews their rating structures in three particular ways. The first is with regard to the subindustry-specific set of factors, which is reviewed on an annual basis. It is at this stage where new indicators may be applied, depending upon what is relevant after the review. At the company level, there is also an annual review. This comprises of an update on company-specific exposures, together with a management assessment. The agency does this by collecting publicly available information, media, and NGO reports. After a robust peer-review process, the third component of the process is applied, which is a continuous assessment driven by the daily news flow. These are ranked by categories and applied as necessary. Finally, the draft report is then sent to companies for their views on the research gathered.

3.2.2 MSCI ESG Scores

For MSCI, their ESG scores are developed by a global team of more than 185 research analysts who assess thousands of data points across 37 key ESG issues. These issues focus on the company's core business and the industry issues that may create risks and opportunities for the company. The companies rated are 'rated on a AAA-CCC scale relative to the standards and performance of their industry peers'.[20] In terms of setting the context for the aims of the ratings, MSCI declare that there are a number of questions that the research analysts seek to answer:

- Of the negative externalities that companies in an industry generate, which issues may turn into unanticipated costs for companies in the medium to long term?
- Conversely, which ESG issues affecting an industry may turn into opportunities for companies in the medium to long term?

More specifically, the MSCI ESG Ratings model seeks to answer four key questions about companies:

- What are the most significant ESG risks and opportunities facing a company and its industry?
- How exposed is the company to those key risks and/or opportunities?
- How well is the company managing key risks and opportunities?
- What is the overall picture for the company and how does it compare to its global industry peers?[21]

MSCI, like Sustainalytics, is quick to declare its views on materiality given its importance to their users. MSCI state that a given risk becomes material when it is 'likely that companies in a given industry will incur substantial costs in connection with it', with the cited example being a regulatory ban on a key chemical input, which then requires reformulation. Interestingly, MSCI also declare when an opportunity may become material, with the focus being on the opportunity to exploit the opportunity for profit; the cited example in this instance is opportunities in clean technology for the LED lighting industry. MSCI identify these potential risks and opportunities via quantitative models that look at ranges and values for each industry and for externalised impacts from issues such as carbon intensity, water intensity, and injury rates. There are further quantitative procedures applied for companies with diversified business models, or who have suffered controversies, etc.

Again, like Sustainalytics, MSCI focus a lot on the management of a company, unsurprisingly. To that end, their quantitative models measure both risk exposure, and risk management. In order to score well, management would need to commensurate with the level of exposure, i.e. appropriate resources applied to the exposure of risk. Companies who are exposed to greater risks and who have strong management structures will score well, whereas those who do not will not score well.

A question that may be raised is how MSCI understand the risk faced by a company. Whilst key issues can be applied at the industry level (and are), the exposure for companies within a given industry may vary. To ascertain the individual exposure, MSCI perform a granular breakdown of a company's business, focusing on elements like its core products or business model, its location(s), and any other relevant factor, like whether they outsource operations and to what level. This is then scored on a 0–10 scale, with 10 representing a high exposure to risk. It is within this 0–10 scale that the company's response to identified risks is factored in, with strong management responses garnering a lowering of the ranking within the 10-point scale.

Moving higher up the process, there are 'Key Issues' that are weighted at the subindustry level. In order to develop and then apply those weightings, MSCI base them on the relative external impact for the subindustry, and also the time horizons associated with each risk. Like Sustainalytics, Corporate Governance is considered heavily and is weighted for all companies. If a company should have company-specific exceptions, then this is removed from the overall weighting applied to companies within the subindustry rating. To arrive at a final letter rating, the 'Weighted Average Key Issue'—which is calculated based upon the underlying Key Issue scores—is then normalised for the industry. MSCI utilise their indexing experience here, by establishing industry scores based upon averaging from the top and bottom scores of constituents within the MSCI ACWI (All Country World Index) Index constituents. As MSCI then confirm:

> Using these ranges, the Weighted Average Key Issue Score is converted to an Industry Adjusted Score from 0-10, where zero is worst and 10 is best. The Industry Adjusted Score corresponds to a rating between best (AAA) and the worst (CCC). These assessments of company performance are not absolute but are explicitly intended to be relative to the standards and performance of a company's industry peers.[22]

MSCI then provide a representation of how the average scores transform into letter ratings[23]:

Letter rating	*Final industry-adjusted company score*
AAA	8.6*–10.0
AA	7.1–8.6
A	5.7–7.1
BBB	4.3–5.7
BB	2.9–4.3
B	1.4–2.9
CCC	0.0–1.4

With regard to collecting information, MSCI has a number of avenues that it utilises. At a macro-level, they use data collected by academics, governments, and/or NGO datasets. To supplement that at the company level, they look at company disclosures like Form 10-Ks, sustainability reports, or AGM results. They also make use of governmental databases, and trawling the business media. In terms of the companies themselves, they are invited participate in the process prior to the publication of the report, in order to verify or put forward any other relevant information. However, there are weekly reports that are available that would allow a company to both see and react to the development of the research on them. The companies are monitored on an ongoing basis, and there is a daily monitoring of any controversies or governance-related events. At each stage of the process, there is an in-depth quality review, with a methodology review committee overseeing the development of the scoring. Lastly, there is a review of the key issues applied to the industries in November of each year, with proposed changes discussed with clients are part of the process.

There is no one representative methodology for the CSS sector, with all of the players having different processes to gather, understand, and then articulate key information. Even the method of articulation is widely different across the sector. If I, as a manager of an institutional investor, wanted to move forward my organisation and start to really incorporate sustainability into my investment processes, which information provider would I use? If I wanted to focus more on the supply chains of companies, and the effect that they may have upon the entity I am investing in, then EcoVadis would be the main contender. But, other than EcoVadis, all other CSSs claim to do the same thing, differently. If I wanted to understand the extent to which a company I am investing in is exposed to ESG-related risks, then how do I know to trust one CSS over the other?

Furthermore, what help is it to me as an Investment manager when one firm tells me that the company is rated as BBB, and another CSS tells me the same company is rated as EEE? I then have to understanding the terminological differences in the two rating scales and, somehow, determine whether the two ratings are actually within the same range of rating. How would I do that, when the methodologies and what underpins them are not made uniformly clear? Even these hypothetical musings demonstrate the difficulties affecting the CSS universe with regard to the mainstream, but there are many more.

3.3 Problems Affecting the CSS Universe

There is no shortage of criticism and identified problems in the literature focusing upon the CSS universe. There may be reasons for this however, particularly when we step back and broaden our perspective. Ignoring Robeco's foundation in 1929 for a moment, one of the earliest entities in the CSS universe was Vigeo-Eiris, and that is because EIRIS was developed as an entity to help inform religious investors *in the 1980s*. That makes the industry less than 40 years old, and in truth the vast majority of the industry only came to be in the 2000s and beyond. This is an incredibly short period of time within which an industry can organise properly to meet its users' demands. Furthermore, their user base as we witness today is even younger still. The 'mainstreamisation' only began after the Financial Crisis, and even then it is still very much in its infancy. Therefore, we have a young industry trying to cater to an even younger market. It is inevitable that divergences exist. Nevertheless, in order to apply to the mainstream, these issues need to be identified and resolved as soon as possible. The identification portion of that dynamic is already well under way.

Escrig-Olmedo helpfully categorises the main issues for us, although there are more. Those main issues are:

(i) Lack of transparency. ESG rating agencies do not offer complete and public information about the criteria and the assessment process developed by them to evaluate the corporate sustainability performance. This makes understanding what ESG rating agencies are measuring and making comparisons between them difficult.
(ii) Commensurability. ESG rating agencies may measure the same concept in different ways. Therefore, if the assessments of

ESG ratings are not consistent, which involves evidence of low commensurability, the hypothesised benefits of CSR cannot occur.

(iii) Trade-Offs among criteria. ESG ratings methodologies may compensate higher scores in one domain with very low scores in another domain.

(iv) Lack of an overall score. Most of the ESG rating agencies provide environmental, social and governance rates to each domain, but they do not provide an overall score of the corporate sustainability performance.

(v) Stakeholders' preferences. ESG rating agencies do not address the different stakeholders' expectations in their evaluation processes, which influences their acceptance and usefulness.[24]

Perhaps one of the clearest and most discussed issues is the concept of measurement and also comparability. Commensurability, which means to have a common measure, is a particular problem. As Escrig-Olmedo et al. note, 'rater continue to have low agreement even when we adjust for explicit differences in what they say they are trying to measure. When commensurability is low, then all or most raters have high measurement error when trying to measure similar theoretical constructs'.[25] The scholars suggest that this calls into the question the very point of these ratings, which is then only exacerbated when we consider the effect that they may potentially have the bigger the mainstreaming of sustainable business practices become.

Berg et al. develop this research and confirm that, in terms of the recognised discrepancies, 53% of identified discrepancies comes from the fact that the CSSs are measuring the same categories *differently*.[26] Furthermore, the researchers find that the incongruencies are not industry- or category-specific, but rater-specific. They call this the 'rater effect', which means that if a company performs better in one particular sector as judged by a CSS, it will perform better in all other sectors too for that same CSS. To further explain this, 'a firm that is perceived as good will be seen through a positive lens and receive better indicator scores than the individual indicator would have allowed for, and vice versa'.[27] In terms of correlation, the researchers find that there are wide differences, evidencing the suggestions from Escrig-Olmedo et al. Remarkably, even categories that are concerned with measuring factual elements, rather than subjective or hard-to-evidence aspects, like membership of the UN Global Compact, or CEO-Chairperson separation, are massively divergent—rates of 0.86 and 0.56 have been found, respectively. It is incredible that a membership to a global initiative can be in question. One reason for this comes in the form of poor issuer disclosure, or it could be the differences in information gathering between the CSS. Either or, but neither is optimal.

Chatterji et al. also find evidence of low correlation and conclude that 'the low agreement implies all or almost all of the ratings have low validity. This result has important implications for managers, investors, and researchers who use these ratings. But if the ratings are not actually valid and cannot consistently identify socially responsible firms, then the hypothesised benefits of CSR cannot occur'.[28] One of the major problems underpinning this divergence is different understandings of concepts that do not have commonly agreed definitions. For example, how does one understand the concept of materiality? Or what *sustainability* even looks like, or consists of? What elements of ESG are more appropriate, or not?

In relating back to a previous point, the nascency of the industry and the market that it is serving is demonstrated in the ever-changing focus of the CSSs themselves. Escrig-Olmedo et al. note that CSS focus has changed massively in the past decade, from focusing on emissions and climate change in 2008 to water usage and management, and protection of biodiversity in 2018. Similar changes across the decade are witnessed across all three of the ESG perspectives.[29] This impacts the development of a standard of 'materiality', both in a financial and non-financial sense.[30] In analysing the published methodological guidance from the CSSs, it was clear that there was a reluctance to declare how materiality was understood by the firm, with a number of platitudes being offered. This reluctance is likely due to the potential problem of putting oneself out in front of one's competitors, particularly when there is no global standard to attach oneself to. If a CSS was the declare an understanding of materiality that was too far away from what investors wanted/could tolerate, then their loss within the marketplace could be substantial given the congested competitive nature of the industry. 'Materiality', as a concept, is derived from the financial accounting arena. It has been transferred and implanted into the sustainability arena, when the reality is that it may not be congruent with the aims of the concept of sustainability. We spoke about this in the last chapter, with the 'mainstreamisation' of the concept being regarded as a dilution of the mission, but the lack of agreement even on the global level is not helping. Eccles et al. note how the two main arbiters of standards in this realm—the Sustainability Accounting

Standards Board (SASB) and the Global Reporting Initiative (GRI)—disagree on what materiality means, with the GRI identifying materiality as an externality, whereas the SASB 'identifies material ESG issues for value-driven investment at the industry level based on their relevance to each firm's financial performance'.[31] The organisations themselves have declared that there should not be a rivalry and that they are merely tools for different purposes, but this simply adds to the complexity in a new environment.[32] These disagreements on basic understandings that need to be foundational in this new field are nothing new,[33] but certainly do not help the progression of the field.

Yet, other elements do not help the progression of the field either. Bias has been widely identified as being a particularly important issue. In addition to the bias described by Berg et al. above, whereby a CSS will positively (or negatively) rate a company across the board if it is perceived as good (or bad), even where such indicators do not allow for it, there are other examples of bias. One is geographical, in the sense that 'in common with investment coverage for all themes of investment and investment research, there is a bias in the current ESG ratings and indexes toward certain geographies, economies, and publicly listed companies because that is where the most readily available research is, and the most demand from investors for company research coverage'.[34] The OECD has also found that companies with sustainable practices are being punished by CSSs for belonging to economies which are not adequately focused upon.[35] This bias, seemingly based on access to information, is replicated at the company level, with larger firms receiving better scores on average, and large swathes of the SME market suffering as a result.[36] The access to data is a particular issue for CSSs, because as the OECD explain 'a lack of consistent corporate disclosure regimes at the international level hinders information available to investors'[37]; this clearly applies to the CSS universe also, who are dependent upon publicly available information.[38]

There are many other methodological based issues. Mountfield et al. note that there is an array of suppliers of information operating within the CSS universe, upon whom the CSSs are very reliant; all of these different informational suppliers have different methodologies themselves, as well as differing terminological foundations for their assimilation of their research[39] (like NGO and Academic datasets—we have seen even in the literature utilised in this chapter the different terminologies for the same concepts/entities). In terms of the rating methodologies themselves, it has been identified that they do not take into account an intergenerational perspective, thereby limiting the authority and validity of the ratings that are supposed to aid long-term thinking investors.[40] There is also an interlinking issue in that researchers have found that CSSs, despite their methodological claims, are starting to focus a lot more on the 'E' and the 'S' and less so the 'G'.[41] This could be because the credit rating agencies dominate the focus and applicability on Governance as part of their creditworthiness assessments, but this should not be the case as ESG principles need to be assessed with equal importance. It has also been recognised, rather widely, that the assessments of the 'E' and 'S' issues are largely subjective, with the 'S'ocial assessments being highlighted as being particularly subjective.[42] Combining these two understandings is worrying for the future of the CSS universe, because if they are starting to focus on elements which are, by definition, very difficult to quantify, their relevance to the mainstream investor base will continue to decline.

The CSS universe is an unenviable position. They are faced with the potential of morphing the future of investment, as well as remarkable riches which, for a nascent industry, cannot be underestimated. However, to date, there is very little evidence that they can meet the demands of the mainstream investor base that requires easy-to-assimilate, comparable, accurate, and objective information. The CSS universe, with its disparate and conflicting organisational structure, is currently incapable of meeting that need. This is not to say, of course, that this will always be the case, but the issue is whether the mainstream will either wait, or tolerate the need to organisationally develop to meet the need. There are market dynamics unfolding that may bring the game towards the CSS universe more, and we shall look at them more closely in Chapters 4 and 5. However, there is an argument that the mainstream need not wait for the CSS universe to organisationally develop to meet their need because, in the credit rating industry, there is already a potentially ready-made, willing, and familiar powerhouse waiting to partake in the feast that will come with the true 'mainstreamisation' of the concept of sustainable investment. It is now time to meet that powerhouse.

Notes

1. Elena Escrig-Olmedo, Maria A. Fernandez-Izquierdo, Idoya Ferrero-Ferrero, Juana M. Rivera-Lirio, and Maria J. Munoz-Torres, 'Rating the Raters: Evaluating How ESG Rating Agencies Integrate Sustainability Principles' (2019) 11 *Sustainability* 917.

2. Borja Diez-Cañamero, Tania Bishara, Jose Ramon Otegi-Olaso, Rikardo Minguez, and José María Fernández, 'Measurement of Corporate Social Responsibility: A Review of Corporate Sustainability Indexes, Rankings and Ratings' (2020) 12 *Sustainability* 2153.
3. (n 1) 921.
4. Michael S. Pagano, Graham Sinclair, and Tina Young, 'Understanding ESG Ratings and ESG Indexes' in Sabri Boubaker, Douglas Cumming, and Duc Khuong Nguyen, *Research Handbook of Finance and Sustainability* (Edward Elgar 2018) 365.
5. David Burrows, 'ESG Ratings: A Call for Consistency' (2020) Institute of Environmental Management and Assessment (Nov 2). https://transform.iema.net/article/esg-ratings-call-consistency (accessed 13/12/20).
6. (n 4) 340.
7. Giovanni Landi and Andrea Tomo, 'The Dark Side of Ethics in Finance: Empirical Evidences from the Italian Market' in Agata Stachowicz-Stanusch, Gianluigi Mangia, Adele Calarelli, and Wolfgang Amann, *Organisational Social Irresponsibility: Tools and Theoretical Insights* (IAP 2017) 164.
8. Aaron K. Chatterji, David I. Levine, and Michael W. Toffel, 'How Well Do Social Ratings Actually Measure Corporate Social Responsibility?' (2009) 18 *Journal of Economics & Management Strategy* 1 126.
9. (n 2) 2154.
10. (n 4) 340.
11. Florian Berg, Julian F. Koelbel, and Roberto Rigobon, 'Aggregate Confusion: The Divergence of ESG Ratings' (2019) MIT Sloan School Working Paper 5822-19, 5.
12. Robert G Eccles, Linda-Eling Lee, and Judith C. Stroehle, 'The Social Origins of ESG: An Analysis of Innovest and KLD' (2019) *Organization & Environment* 1.
13. Daniel Cash, 'Sustainable Rating Agencies' in Magdalena Ziolo, *Finance and Sustainable Development: Designing Sustainable Financial Systems* (Routledge 2021) 149.
14. Ali Shahzad, Nicholas Bartoski, Brandi K. McManus, and Mark P. Sharfman, 'A Researcher's Guide to Business and Society Archival Datasets' in Abagail McWilliams, Deborah E. Rupp, Donald S. Siegel, Gunter K. Stahl, and David A. Waldman, *The Oxford Handbook of Corporate Social Responsibility* (Oxford: Oxford University Press 2019) 552.
15. Daniel Cash, *Regulation and the Credit Rating Agencies: Restraining Ancillary Services* (Routledge 2018).
16. CDP, *Companies Scores* (2020). https://www.cdp.net/en/companies/companies-scores.

17. Sustainalytics, *The ESG Risk Ratings: Methodology-Abstract Version 2.0* (2019) 4. https://connect.sustainalytics.com/hubfs/INV%20-%20Reports%20and%20Brochure/Methodology/Sustainalytics_ESG%20Risk%20Rating_Methodology%20Abstract_Nov2019.pdf (accessed 14/12/2020).
18. Ibid. 5.
19. Ibid. 9.
20. MSCI, *MSCI ESG Ratings Methodology* (MSCI 2019) 2. https://www.msci.com/documents/1296102/14524248/MSCI+ESG+Ratings+Methodology+-+Exec+Summary+2019.pdf/2dfcaeee-2c70-d10b-69c8-3058b14109e3?t=1571404887226 (accessed 14/12/2020).
21. Ibid. 3.
22. Ibid. 11.
23. Ibid.
24. (n 1) 921.
25. Ibid. 1608.
26. (n 11) 4.
27. Ibid. 28.
28. Aaron Chatterji, Rodolphe Durand, David I. Levine, and Samuel Touboul, 'Do Ratings of Firm Converge? Implications for Managers, Investors and Strategy Researchers' (2016) 37 *Strategic Management Journal* 8 1598, 1597–1614.
29. (n 1) 925.
30. OECD, *OECD Business and Finance Outlook 2020 Sustainable and Resilient Finance* (OECD Publishing 2020) 28.
31. (n 12) 5.
32. Tim Mohinof and Jean Rogers, 'SASB and GRI Pen Joint Op-Ed on Sustainability Reporting Synchronicity' (2017). https://www.sasb.org/blog/blog-sasb-gri-pen-joint-op-ed-sustainability-reporting-sychronicity/ (accessed 14/12/2020).
33. Alex C. Michalos, 'The Business Case for Asserting the Business Case for Business Ethics' (2013) 114 *Journal of Business Ethics* 4 605.
34. (n 4) 359.
35. (n 30) 29.
36. Ibid.; (n 4) 339.
37. (n 3) 28.
38. Samuel Drempetic, Christian Klein, and Bernhard Zwergel, 'The Influence of Firm Size on the ESG Score: Corporate Sustainability Ratings Under Review' (2019) *Journal of Business Ethics* 1 16.
39. Andrew Mountfield, Matthew Gardner, Bernd Kasemir, and Stephan Lienin, 'Integrated Management for Capital Markets and Strategy: The Challenges of "Value" Versus "Values" Sustainability Investment, Smart Bet, and Their Consequences for Corporate Leadership' in Thomas Wunder, *Rethinking Strategic Management: Sustainable Strategizing for Positive Impact* (Springer 2019) 114.

40. (n 1) 928.
41. María Jesús Muñoz-Torres, María Ángeles Fernández-Izquierdo, Juana M. Rivera-Lirio, and Elena Escrig-Olmedo, 'Can Environmental, Social, and Governance Rating Agencies Favour Business Models That Promote a More Sustainable Development? (2019) 26 *Corporate Social Responsibility and Environmental Management* 447.
42. (n 11) 19.

CHAPTER 4

The Credit Rating Agencies

The credit rating industry has become a central component of the financial architecture over the years. Whilst this has not always been the case for the predominant 'Big Three' credit rating agencies of Standard & Poor's (now S&P Global), Moody's, and Fitch Ratings, there were reasons for this—the important aspect to understand is that their *role* has been central to the financial architecture for nearly 200 years in various guises. The question for our analysis here is whether that role will be central to the new financial architecture, one theoretically based upon sustainability and forward-thinking finance.

The leading credit rating agencies have, since the Financial Crisis, been jostling for supremacy ahead of the predicted 'mainstreamisation' of the concept of sustainable finance and investment. The acquiring of data service companies has been continuing at a rapid pace and shows absolutely no signs of slowing down; at the time of writing, S&P are poised to make the biggest purchase of a company in 2020 globally, reportedly agreeing to spend $44 billion on acquiring HIS Markit.[1] If this acquisition goes through as expected, then it will be further evidence of the concerted approach the credit rating giants are taking.

However, what does this approach mean? Does it really put the credit rating industry in the best position to serve the mainstreamisation of sustainable business/finance/investment? Is that even their aim? To find out, there are a number of things we can focus on. The main aspect

D. Cash, *Sustainability Rating Agencies vs Credit Rating Agencies*, Palgrave Studies in Impact Finance,
https://doi.org/10.1007/978-3-030-71693-6_4

we will focus on in this chapter is the declarations from the Big Three regarding how they are integrating ESG into their rating methodologies. Like the CSSs, there is a lot of lip-service and platitudes on offer but, as opposed to the CSSs, the credit rating agencies are mandated by law to publicly detail their methodological processes. This has led to an array of information from the Big Three agencies which will be particularly useful for us. We shall also examine the M&A activity alongside this analysis, to contextualise the development of what the Big Three are offering and will no doubt continue to add to. However, in order to truly understand the agencies and be able to best predict what may come next, we need to really know the rating agencies inside and out.

4.1 The Credit Rating Picture

The credit rating agencies have a long and storied history. Before them came the credit *referencing* agencies, whom I have argued consistently must be considered when looking at the historical trajectory of the modern-day agencies. There have been a number of key works within the literature that have charted the history,[2] and the constitution of the credit rating industry,[3] so that we have a fuller picture of this incredibly impactful industry. There are inconsistencies within the lineage of the literature unfortunately, but they are easily corrected. In this section, we shall get to know the credit rating agencies and what they do by depending upon this lineage as cited above.

Credit rating agencies, theoretically, have a very simple purpose. They are relied upon to opine on the creditworthiness of a given entity; namely, how likely is one to receive their investment back, in full, and on time? Obviously, given how the global economy has evolved since the first commercialised agencies were founded, the role of the modern credit rating agencies has evolved with it. Whether that evolution was because the marketplace required it, or the rating agencies evolved with the times to take advantage, is something we shall discuss later in the chapter. However, their role is indeed very simple indeed. The agencies theoretically sit in the middle of a number of dynamic arrangements and serve a number of entities as a result. Let us think very simply for a moment. How may I as a small investor know what may constitute a good investment amongst the myriad of investable opportunities? The credit ratings provided by the leading agencies are actually free of charge for the most part, so it is of direct help to the retail investor. If I, as an investor, am invested in an institutional investor, how may I seek to either know, or even constrain the investment managers in charge of my fund? If I and other investors were to set constraints on those managers in order to protect my underlying investment, a third-party and technically independent source of easy-to-assimilate and understand ratings on investments would be ideal, What if I, as a regulator, have been tasked with restraining the actions of banking institutions and require them only to invest in the safest of investments because of the systemic risk their activities carry? How would I even know, or be able to articulate to other parties, what constitutes a *safe* investment? If I were an issuer who needed to obtain finance for a new project, or just to become more liquid, how would I signal to investors that I am worth investing in, and that they are likely to receive their investment back, and on time? What if I am a genuinely responsible and prudent business seeking finance, but one of my competitors has performed badly and is in distress—why should I have to pay the same rates of interest as my competitor?

You can see from these questions above that there is a *systemic* need for the credit rating agencies. There have been many that have argued that credit ratings do not hold much, if any informational value but that, instead, they serve other purposes or enjoy success because of other dynamics.[4] Partnoy is potentially the biggest proponent of the concept of rating agencies only being successful because regulators have granted 'regulatory licences' which are proving hard to remove.[5] I have argued against this 'regulatory licence' theory, by proposing that instead the reason that the agencies are so prevalent is because they are in receipt of a 'market licence',[6] i.e. the market needs what they offer and allows their practices on that basis. I agree with Partnoy that informational value is not what the market requires from the agencies, necessarily, but rather an array of other purposes, including the need to *signal* and bypass informational asymmetry in the theoretical sense. It will be worth keeping this sentiment in mind as we progress through the trajectory of the agencies.

4.1.1 The Trajectory of a Binding Relationship

The common thought in the literature when looking at the trajectory of the rating industry is to start with the company that John Moody founded in 1900, and work our way forwards. Whilst that may be technically correct, because his was the first *credit rating agency*, it does not exactly tell the full story nor contextualise the industry's development well enough. To understand why I propose the concept of a 'market licence' rather than a 'regulatory licence', it is important to understand a. what happened before the first 'regulatory licence' was developed in the 1930s, and why the products that were offered either succeeded or failed.

The first form of formally collating data on businesses in order to understand better their creditworthiness was in the UK, with Scottish and English 'Mercantile Societies' forming to provide members with protection against 'swindlers and sharpers'.[7] This process in the Eighteenth and Nineteenth centuries was crucially important because of the lack of any creditor protection. These were not commercialised entities, but rather societies that members contributed to. The creditor protection that a lot of the developed world enjoys today was absolutely absent during this period, and that clearly plays a part in the development of creditworthiness assessment. However, as European nations began establishing bankruptcy networks and associated protections, the nascent American economy widely rejected such notions and, even more so, a rejection of large foreign banking entities conducting business in the country.[8] According to the literature, the next major development within the trajectory of this process centred around the expansion of the modern-day U.S., with wealthy European banking entities facing the prospect of dealing with more people who they were not accustomed to dealing with. The Baring Brothers banking entity is perhaps the clearest example of this problem, and their solution provides a template for what was to come. In the early 1800s, Baring Brothers wanted to survey the creditworthiness of American Houses and opportunities, and hired Thomas Wren Ward—'a retired, well to do merchant from Boston'—to utilise his experience and connections to rank local businesspeople, whether or not they had been asked to be included, on a scale from 1 to 11. He developed a formal network to achieve this objective and his approach was noted for its remarkable accuracy given the amount of data available and the volatility of the marketplace.[9]

However, as Wren and his team grew older, their tolerance for younger entrants to the marketplace grew less. This led to the team being regarded as 'antediluvian' in their approach.[10] The process adopted by the team was well known on the East Coast of the United States and, in 1835, the first commercialised entity was established by the Law firm of Griffen, Cleaveland, and Campbell in New York City. The firm developed a 'network of attorneys throughout the city' that produced reports on businesspeople which subscribers could view at the offices of the firm whenever they wished.[11] However, in the mid-1830s the US economy as experiencing a 'heady economic boom' that reduced the appetite for credit risk analysis, and the Law firm soon folded. Nevertheless, a pious businessman and Lawyer named Lewis Tappan, famed for representing the rebellious slaves on board the schooner *La Amistad*, picked up the pieces of the failed business and started to put together a more formal business. What happened next is up for debate, but either via insight, luck, or another reason, him timing could not have been better. The antebellum U.S. suffered a number of economic crises, and the Panic of 1837 was chief amongst them. The Panic led to a rapid changing of the mentality within the country, from legislators at least, and the newly elected Whig Congress responded by enacting *The National Bankruptcy Act of 1841*. The Act 'sought to provide relief to the thousands of individuals who had failed during the dramatic deflation that followed the Panics of 1837 and 1839'.[12] Whilst Congress had sought to provide relief, the reaction was one of fear, particularly the fear that the Act allowed 'sharpsters' to escape their debts; the worry was that the Act amounted to a 'jubilee' or a 'universal pardoning of all debt'. This fear increased the public's appetite for credit risk assessment and, right on time, Tappan launched the *Mercantile Agency* just two days after the Act was enacted. Coincidentally, the Act was repealed just thirteen months later.[13]

Tappan and the Agency's development is particularly fascinating, and features a story of incredible business acumen, betrayal, legal oppression, regret, racism, and scandal.[14] For our purposes, it is worth noting the Agency's model. It was, by definition, a *referencing* approach rather than a *rating* approach. The Agency perfected the approach that had been taken by Griffen, Cleaveland, and Campbell, with the Agency consisting of lawyers all over the U.S. who would report on local business entities (famed reporters included Abraham Lincoln and Ulysses S. Grant before their time in the Presidential Office); the reports were held centrally in New York City and, for a subscription fee, one could peruse the reports. The Agency's main competitor at the time was John Bradstreet's company *The Bradstreet Co.*, and it was the Bradstreet Company that moved the art further, pioneering the Reference Book, which could be sent out to subscribers rather than have subscribers attend the central office. The Reference Book even included 'notification sheets' which were an addendum and brought their references right up to date (the original rating modifiers). This moved the process towards more of a *ranking* process. At the same time, the two leading referencing entities were being exposed to a variety of legal challenges against their right to publish such information, with the common argument being that negative reports were libellous. Interestingly, the Courts predominantly sided with the agencies and ruled that their reports constituted 'opinions' protected under the Constitution. This is what Flandreau and his colleagues label as the granting of a 'legal license', but which is essentially based upon a 'market licence' in that the market wanted, and in essence *needed* the agencies and their products to deal with the asymmetry that was creeping into the ever-expanding U.S.

In the literature, there is virtually no linkage between the reference and rating industries, apart from much later on when the merged Dun and Bradstreet purchased Moody's (we shall look at that shortly). However, that is not actually the case. The *rating* agencies were not direct competitors for the *referencing* agencies as the former came later, but there are linkages. Henry Varnum Poor had published his *History of Railroads and Canals in the United States* in 1860, but he did not form his company *H.V. and H.W. Poor* until 1867, and the company did not form into *Poor's Railroad Manual Company* until much later on.[15] Henry's wife was Tappan's niece, and it is understood that he took inspiration for his business structures and rating approaches from Tappan himself.[16] In 1900, John Moody founded his first company *John Moody & Co*, which published *Moody's Manual of Industrial and Miscellaneous Securities*[17]; however, the venture was to be short-lived because, as a result of the stock market downturn in 1903, he lost control of the company and its name. Yet, Moody was not down for long and, with the help of R.G. Dun & Co., the *Mercantile Agency* under a new name and owner (Robert G. Dun), John Moody established the *Analyses Publishing Co.* in 1907 and his new idea was revolutionary for the industry: he now focused on rating *securities*, as well as companies. He launched *Moody's Analyses of Investments* in 1910 and the 'rating' industry began to take shape as we know it. For its modern-day rival S&P, Poor's merged with Standard Statistics—founded itself in 1906 as the Standard Statistics Bureau by Luther Lee Blake—in 1941 after Poor's ran into financial difficulties.[18] Coincidentally, Blake hired Moody for a year after he lost control of his first company. As noted earlier, Dun and Bradstreet would purchase Moody's in 1962 because of Moody's suffering similar financial difficulties.

This malaise would continue up unto the late 1960s when the credit rating agencies would, relatively, explode back onto the scene. The dominant view in the literature is that this relatively rapid growth was because, in 1973, the Securities and Exchange Commission essentially began the era of forcing the rating agencies upon the financial markets, which would accumulate into the act of registering 'recognised' rating agencies via the moniker of being a 'Nationally Recognised Statistical Rating Organisation' (NRSRO). I and others have shown this to be not entirely true, on two fronts. Flandreau and his colleagues' work has shown that the reliance upon the agencies, from the perspective of regulators and the judiciary, started well before 1933 with the Securities Acts, as the dominant argument goes—the sentiment is that reliance was started in the 1930s and then cemented in the 1970s, thus establishing a 'regulatory licence'. With regard to the importance of the NRSRO designation, I have shown that this was, in fact, a *reactive* measure (as the regulatory approaches in the 1930s were) to the marketplace and its dynamics, rather than a *proactive* regulatory approach as has been claimed.[19]

Very briefly, the established narrative argues that the credit rating agencies lost relevance because the market was doing so well, that people did not require risk assessments (and that they trusted brands and businesses generally) a la pre-1841. After the Penn Central railroad conglomerate defaulted on its commercial paper, investors were left shocked and at a loss, and turned to the credit rating agencies as their appetite for risk assessment increased. Then, the SEC cemented their position by pushing the agencies onto the market. In reality, this is not the case. The market *was* using methods for assessing risk, they just chose another entity—namely, the *National Credit Office* that was an offshoot of Dun and Bradstreet. The National Credit Office were providing their highest ratings for commercial paper across the board and, like the aftermath of the Financial Crisis, the SEC found numerous examples of conflicts of interest and fraud within this process after the highly rated Penn Central defaulted on its Commercial Paper.[20] Therefore, the market needed a third-party verifier of creditworthiness just like it always had, and they moved more towards the credit rating agencies in the aftermath of the collapse because they were all that were left. This sequence of events is actually one of the strongest examples of the 'market licence' argument, and of the bind that exists between the market and the credit rating agencies, rather than a footnote in the history of the agencies as the dominant narrative in the literature prescribes.

The rating industry developed steadily from that point onwards, although not dramatically. S&P developed under the auspices of its parent company McGraw-Hill, and Warren Buffett's Berkshire Hathaway bought

Dun and Bradstreet in 2000, and immediately spun the Moody's brand off; they maintained their control of Moody's as a now stand-alone entity, and sold Dun and Bradstreet, meaning they paid just $5.56 per share for control of what is now a multi-billion dollar company.[21] Whilst the auditing profession took the bulk of the regulatory glare after the failures of Enron and WorldCom, the credit rating agencies themselves would be regulated for the first time in their history in 2005 and then 2006,[22] although it was to be too late to stop the financial catastrophe that was about to engulf the world in 2007 and 2008.

The reason why the credit rating agencies were catapulted into the public consciousness during and after the Crisis was because of their pivotal role in allowing the financial mechanisms that caused the downturn to function. The process underpinning the securitised residential mortgage-backed instruments is called 'asset securitisation' and involves the pooling of a category of loans into one large pool that is then sold to investors in different sectors. The interest and principal payments of the underlying loans are fed into one stream, and where an investor sits down that stream to collect is dependent upon their appetite for risks; theoretically, the surer returns offer less return, whilst the riskier rates of return allow for the greatest level of return. This is all divided by 'tranche' (French for 'slice') and, in order to determine these credit levels, credit rating agencies were supposed to evaluate the *underlying* loans to establish the creditworthiness of each tranche. The more risk-averse, or regulatory constrained investors like institutional investors (because of the systemic risk their failures would create), were constrained to invest only in the senior tranches. After that came the mezzanine tranches, within which insurance companies were investing. Lastly, in the 'equity' tranches, the hedgefunds invested, because of their appetite for risk and returns, and their lack of regulatory constraint. The theory was that losses stemming from the underlying pool of loans—say, via delinquencies on mortgage payments—would be felt on an escalating scale, from the bottom up.[23]

Investors from around the world invested in this process, all underpinned by two particular factors: the Government-backed entities of Fannie Mae and Freddie Mac were allowing for more and more people to access cheap funding for the purchase of homes; and, these products were receiving the highest of ratings from the credit rating agencies. The rating agencies were vouching for the *underlying* pool of assets, so there was technically very little chance of the senior tranches being affected by what would only ever be a small amount of delinquencies, which would be absorbed by the equity tranches. In theory, it spreads the risk and allows for risk appetite to be catered for. However, whilst investors have always been told to do their due diligence before investing, this process was offering returns that were too tempting to ignore and, when combined with the highest ratings possible, the perfect storm was complete. Yet, the credit rating agencies did not know about the underlying issues within the asset pool—wide instances of mortgage fraud and poor lending practices were rife across the asset pool—and even worse were actively developing tailored methodologies to create the desired ratings for continued investments from the world's largest and most systemically important financial institutions.[24] Even worse still, the leading credit rating agencies actively sided with issuers and had stakes in Special Investment Vehicles that profited greatly from this process.[25]

When this all came to light after the height of the Financial Crisis, the line was drawn in the sand. Never again would the credit rating agencies be able to act without serious regulatory restraint. In the U.S., the Dodd-Frank Act dedicated an entire chapter to overhauling the credit rating industry, adopting rules relating to increasing competition, increased transparency regarding methodologies and rating actions, increased availability for information, and the removal of references to the required use of the ratings within regulations across the financial sector.[26] In Europe, the legislators sought to go even further, particularly as the credit rating agencies had compounded their effect upon the continent by downgrading a number of European countries' sovereign ratings en masse, causing systemic issues that threatened to topple the bloc itself. The E.U. enacted three cumulative pieces of legislation that contained relatively similar actions as the Dodd-Frank Act (although, as we shall see later, the E.U. have really pushed on with regard to controlling the credit rating agencies).[27]

In 2015, new and unwanted records would start to be set for the credit rating agencies. S&P, as a result of its conduct leading up to the Financial Crisis, settled with the US Department of Justice for $1.4bn, and similarly settled with CalPERS for $125 m for the same misdemeanours. Though as part of the settlement S&P did not have to admit wrongdoing, the allegations that the company had defrauded investors was damning; then-Attorney General Eric Holder announced that 'the settlement we have reached today not only makes clear that this kind of conduct will never ben tolerated by the Department of Justice – it also underscores our strong and ongoing commitment to pursue any company or entity that violated the law and contributed to the financial crisis of 2008'.[28] He was not wrong. In 2018, Moody's suffered the same fate and settled for $864 m. If you are wondering why only the Big Two were indicted, and not Fitch Ratings—the third member of the imbalanced oligopoly—it is because they settled with CalPERS earlier on (who had initiated the legal action), not for money but rather for damning evidence that would then be used against the top two targets. This process was developed as part of the Dodd-Frank Act, whereby liability for their credit ratings could finally be properly applied, as long as enough material evidence was provided.

So, why did we need to know all this? I could have easily moved straight into the credit rating agencies' incorporation of ESG into their credit rating processes, as we shall do next. We are interested in the 'battle' between the two industries with regard to serving the ever-growing mainstream investor base and its desire to consider ESG more in its investment practices. If I had just considered their methodological developments over the past few years, then you as the reader would have been able to understand how that development may progress into conflict with the CSS industry. But, there is something more important to understand, and that understanding can only be obtained by considering the underlying purpose of the credit rating agencies. We can only understand this purpose by looking, in close detail, at the trajectory of the agencies through their history. Furthermore, that detail *must* include a *full* account of the history of the providers of the service that the agencies provide, not just the agencies. Not doing so sells an incomplete picture. For example, if we do not consider the National Credit Office, we do not understand why the agencies rebounded into relevancy in the 1960/1970s. If we do not understand what comes before John Moody's first company, then it appears that the engrained culture starts there. It does not. The lineage of the current powerhouses is long and storied, and there are so many effects of that reality.

Nevertheless, the Financial Crisis was a turning point. The credit rating agencies often operated under the public radar. To be in existence for more than 100 years (and longer still considering the *Reference* agencies) and not be regulated formally is some going. Now, that environment no longer exists. The actions of the rating agencies make newspaper headlines. With that alteration in their environment, the rules of engagement have changed. In response to their record settlements and newfound and unwanted public attention, the credit rating agencies' future had to develop and, either by choice, luck, or happenstance, it has. Now, the agencies are being fundamentally aligned to the development of the sustainable investment movement. The UN's Principles of Responsible Investment has partnered with the Big Three to push for them to be as involved as they can be. After a slow start, presumably because of wanting to see how the movement would develop, the Big Three are now really hitting their stride with regard to marketing their developments, acquiring related service providers, trying to be more transparent about how they incorporate ESG into their rating actions, and the importance of data availability in general. Almost synergistically, as the movement grows the credit rating agencies are growing alongside it. It makes sense for them to do this, but as we have seen in this section, the agencies are primed for this; *surviving* irrespective of the environment around them is what they do. They have also correctly realised that investors within the sustainable investment movement *need* certain elements, and the agencies are keen to display that they can provide, because the rewards for doing so could be beyond anything the agencies have seen before.

4.2 The Credit Rating Agencies and ESG

The credit rating agencies' connection to ESG is multifaceted and directly linked to the post-Crisis trajectory. Traditionally, whilst the credit rating agencies may claim (as they do) that ESG has always been factored into their ratings, they have never been under pressure to articulate how and when. The staple for the credit rating agencies has always been credit risk based on the financial fundamentals. When ESG was a factor, it had to be clear and obvious; to publish credit actions on, say, a coal-producing company, would require some mention of the environment and any related environmental regulations etc., for example. Yet, the decision to decide what was 'material', and when to say so, was always on the credit rating agencies' terms.

The Financial Crisis changed that, and in many ways. We shall look more at the concept of 'signalling' in the next chapter, but the concept helps clarify the environmental pressures affecting market participants since the Crisis. Essentially, reputational capital took a massive, once-in-a-generation hit during the Crisis. The transferring of the financial pain to the taxpayer across the Western World (and beyond) via 'quantitative easing' instantaneously impacted upon the reputation of all those involved. As a result, the natural reaction was to seek to repair the damage, although to what degree depended upon how comfortable one was in their systemic position. This is widely understood, as is one of the best ways to improve one's corporate reputation, which is to demonstrate how proactive, caring, and in modern parlance, how *sustainable* one is. This was a common strategy that was employed after the Crisis.[29]

If we think of the societal environment, the aspects that are associated with ESG will naturally be more appealing to the wider society, and therefore corporates, *after* a systemic failure. The justification for spending resources on making the corporate entity have a better impact for more than just the shareholders, should receive a better reception after a breakdown and that is exactly what happened.[30] The turn towards ESG was seen as the 'recoupling' of the marketplace to the 'real economy', moving away from speculation and overvaluation.[31] But, all of this cannot just be a narrative after such a systemic failure. There needs to be a system in place in which the actual uptake of this approach is communicated to relevant others; it needs to be *signalled*.[32]

The CSS universe is one way of signalling that information, which is the reason why we are focusing on them in this book. But, the credit rating agencies are also an incredibly relevant tool. However, that is not necessarily because their signalling is true or to be believed, but that it allows larger processes to continue. The credit rating agencies have been active in describing that they do integrate ESG into their processes anyway, so they are a natural fit for this role. Yet, studies suggest otherwise. Not only is the integration in question—it has been strongly suggested that only the 'G' element has ever been integrated properly, and even then, the rate of integration is questionable[33]—but also it has been argued that the integration of ESG has very little impact, if any, on the accuracy of credit ratings.[34] If that is the case, then why would investors *want* to work with rating agencies and encourage their usage more? There are many answers for that, and we will cover them over the final two chapters. However, we need to look at whether this is actually the case, and also what the credit rating agencies have to say for themselves. To do that we will use two streams of information. The first will be to assess what the issues are in this particular section of the field, via the work conducted by the UN's PRI. Then, we shall look at what the agencies themselves say about ESG and their associated methodologies, in order to ascertain whether they are genuinely committed to the development of the mission, or parasitically along for the ride and the mainstream takes shape.

4.2.1 *The Principles for Responsible Investment*

The UN's Principles for Responsible Investment, launched in 2005 and has the expressed goal of creating a sustainable financial system that can benefit society and the environment, as well as create long-term value. One of the factors within the financial system that they are concerning themselves with is the development of the credit rating industry and its connection to the concept of sustainable/responsible investment. To aid that development, they created a Credit Risk and Ratings Initiative, which 'aims to enhance the transparent and systemic integration of ESG factors in credit risk analysis'. To do this, the Initiative partnered with a number of credit rating agencies—now more than 20—and more than 160 investors to increase the dialogue between the two parties.[35]

I have been both praising and critical of the PRI in the past.[36] I have praised the ambition and the approach of increasing dialogue at such a high and respected level, but criticised the ceding to the credit rating agencies and their position; I believe that the aim is to proactively engage and subsequently improve the conduct of the credit rating agencies, not legitimise their actions. Others have also been critical. Eccles mused whether the ethical elements of the underlying process of responsible finance have been diluted too much by the PRI,[37] ultimately going further when concluding that there is nothing 'responsible' about the PRI's approach and to suggest otherwise 'is at best naive and at worst misrepresentation of the truth'.[38] Kotsantonis et al. suggest that the ever-growing number of signatories to the PRI is a misleading indicator of the take up of responsible investing as a sentiment/approach/mentality; 'the reality is that PRI signatories commit only to behaving in accordance with a set of principles for responsible investment, a commitment that falls short of integrating ESG considerations into all their investment decisions'.[39]

Whilst there has been criticism of the initiative, its potential is clear. Its potential as a global instigator of movement in this particular arena, as well as across the financial sector, is perhaps unrivalled.[40] It may also be the case that we expect too much of the PRI and that it has different aims that fit with a more granular approach, as James Gifford one of the PRI's founders described: 'the important thing is to get people in the tent, for whatever reason. Then once they are in, you can start to inspire change'.[41] Whether or not they are meeting what is expected of them from outsiders, they have been working on increasing dialogue between the rating agencies and investors via a number of vehicles. In terms of articulating that to the public, there have been three extensive reports which are well worth considering, all under the master title of *Shifting Perceptions*.

In the first of the three reports, entitled *The State of Play*, the PRI declare that 'incorporating ESG considerations into credit risk analysis is not a tick-box exercise due to the multi-faceted nature of credit risk is related to the likelihood of default by an issuer'.[42] This is adjoined to the declared understanding that 'not all ESG factors which may affect bonds' price performance influence an issuer's creditworthiness'. The narrative points towards difficulties in the process of integrating ESG into credit risk assessments, and the report categorises these issues under the title of so-called 'disconnects' between parties, and the process. The credit rating agencies see these disconnects and shortcomings as existing in the area of disclosure and transparency, whilst the investor signatories agree and see many more issues.[43]

One of the most significant issues identified was the time horizon that credit rating agencies believe affects materiality. Credit rating agencies argue that the longer the time horizon, the more inaccurate, and ultimately immaterial an ESG-related issue becomes. Investors acknowledged that this was the case, but subsequently argued that because credit rating agencies do not view and articulate ESG risks as a separate category, this issue of the appropriate time horizon and the associated materiality is not visible within ratings. Therefore, one of the clearest requests was for credit rating agencies to overtly weight the ESG factors in their methodologies. The PRI noted that investors tended to align their views on what constituted an acceptable time horizon with their investment objectives, which of course cannot be replicated by the credit rating agencies. Whilst this is to be expected, an issue that was highlighted by an investor was that the credit rating agencies do not update their credit ratings frequently enough to allow for the difference in understanding of time horizon to be bridged. In response, the credit rating agencies all argued that credit ratings for corporates and structured finance tend to have shorter time horizons than any time it would take for ESG issues to materialise; therefore, they are not ignoring ESG when it may appear so, it is just that what they consider to be an appropriate time horizon is shorter than the crystallisation of ESG issues.

The investors asked for the role of credit rating agencies to be replicated in their analysis. For example, whilst not asking for credit rating agencies to foresee and price in so-called Black Swan events, a number of investors argued that credit rating agencies should highlight the ESG issues affecting an issuer *irrespective* of whether the crystallisation of those issues would be later than the time horizon of the rating; the argument goes that the access to non-public information via the issuer-pays model should be leveraged to increase the amount of information in the system. Even if not related to a riskiness of a particular bond, it may be helpful for an investor to know if an issuer *may* be affected by ESG-related issues in the future (thus allowing longer-term investors the ability to understand better the entity they are investing in). As one investor neatly explained:

> I don't completely agree with the statement that CRAs have systemically factored ESG criteria into their methodology. There is scope to better capture indirect, embedded ESG risks which are value/supply chain related... such risks appear to be increasing so may be more investment relevant going forward than in the past.

Interestingly, the topic of regulation comes up frequently during the report. US and E.U. regulations focused on competition (which we will see in the next chapter is a flawed regulatory objective in this field) and transparency. The push was on making the methodological process more transparent, and now registered credit rating agencies must make public their rating methodologies, or at least what impacts its design. However, in highlighting how the regulations are not aligned with the investors' needs, they decry the fact that whilst methodologies are made public, what actually impacted upon each rating is not. The PRI state that this is one of the major difficulties, mostly because a credit rating is made up of both quantitative and qualitative indicators, and thus can be somewhat subjective. Then, when ESG issues are included, the rate of subjectivity naturally increases, particularly when aspects such as 'S' elements are considered.

The report concluded by reaffirming its aims, particularly the aim of increasing dialogue between the two parties. The second report, entitled *Exploring the Disconnects*, endeavoured to provide more detail to the identified 'disconnects' in order to find potential solutions. Published in 2018, the report was set against the backdrop of the unwinding of Quantitative Easing programmes, which is significant because, as the PRI state:

> It also comes as the need to better assess credit risk in line with fundamentals is intensifying with the ongoing unwinding of quantitative monetary policy easing (QE) in several large countries. Yields are normalising after an unprecedented compression which boosted risk appetite and demand for high-yield (low credit-rated) investments in search for income. As a result, the case for identify red flags to price risks more adequately has become more compelling.[44]

The latest approach of the PRI was to put together 'roundtables' of credit rating agency representatives and signatory investor representatives, to move the conversation towards potential solutions. From these roundtable sessions, there were a number of instances of the two parties continuing to advance their position, although there was more compromise displayed by both sides. The biggest issue that the credit rating agencies, and the PRI wanted to make clear was that 'incorporating ESG consideration in credit risk analysis should not be confused with investment strategies that target social or environmental returns in addition to a financial return'. This is symbolic of the jostling for position within the initiative, in that the credit rating agencies consistently attempted, with high levels of success, to define the parameters for what ESG consideration means in practice; it is in their interests to clearly define the restrictions to the concept, in order to limit their exposure to the claim that they are not adequately recognising ESG in their 'opinions'.

Other key outcomes of the roundtables were that the sentiment of ESG just being utilised to identify and price risks had evolved to the understanding that it could help in generating alpha. This frames the conversation very differently and impressed upon all parties that there is a further incentive to engaging in such investment strategies. The credit rating agencies made clear that one of the biggest hurdles they face is to develop a more quantitative, and therefore comparable, ESG framework with which they could develop their rating actions. This understanding was widely shared as the lack of standards and definitions for what ESG-based investing actually constitutes continues to frustrate. In a connected issue, it was also highlighted that there is no accepted method for verifying the impact of ESG-related information.

The report concluded by, in my opinion, placing the responsibility at the feet of the investors. It was made abundantly clear that investors had not been engaging with the informational materials the CRAs had been producing, and those non-US signatories had not heard of sectoral developments, like that of the work of the Sustainability Accounting Standards Board (SASB).

The final report, entitled *From Disconnects to Action Areas*, attempts to develop clear pathways for development in this area. Underneath the content of the report, there is a further developed compromise on display, although the investor body has fought back somewhat against the position of the rating agencies. The investors call for more work to be done by credit rating agencies in terms of making clear their views on the materiality of ESG aspects, with one example request being that colour coding, or heatmapping, could facilitate the effective dissemination of the credit rating agencies' understandings of ESG impact.[45] This should be aligned to a more sophisticated backtesting approach from the credit rating agencies in the opinion of the investors, because whilst they acknowledge that it is not always possible to efficiently backtest historically with regard to ESG impacts, etc., any trends may be appropriate for the future creditworthiness of the entity and the investors believe that such potentially vital information should become a norm in the industry. Also, if an ESG factor is not deemed to be relevant by the credit rating agencies, which the investors seemingly accept is up to the agencies, scenarios in which it may become relevant should be detailed as part of their overarching analysis.

In foreshadowing a discussion that will be detailed more in the final chapter, there are culturally different approaches to instigating change in this arena being displayed across the globe. In the U.S., the most favoured approach is to let the market encourage this change, with institutional investors generally being highlighted as the arbiters for that change. Interestingly, the investors do not categorically agree with that understanding and, correctly, proclaim that the rating agencies have a role to play in developing that change also, mostly on account of their access to issuers and the systemically-central role that they play. As described by the PRI:

> CRAs, by contrast, cannot influence a rated entity's policies or structure, and cannot provide professional or legal advice, but they should engage on ESG topics, when relevant, to assess how a rated entity's management and governance could impact its creditworthiness. Either way, having these conversations more frequently will help issuers to recognise that disregarding material ESG risks can result in suboptimal investments and ratings that could affect their cost of capital. Improved transparency with

> issuers around what investors and CRAs believe are the most material ESG factors to credit risk could also prompt indirect market benefits in terms of improved issuer disclosure and reporting, as well as fostering a market standard of comparable, meaningful metrics that facilitates relative analysis.[46]

The investors do not stop there. They insist that credit rating agencies need to be more explicit in their articulation of how ESG factors impacting upon credit rating actions, and to what extent. In response, the only aspects that the credit rating agencies countered with were twofold: first, that investors need to understand better what ESG consideration is, and not to confuse the process with more traditional approaches like impact investing, and second that the investors need to engage more with the rating agencies and their published information on how they integrate ESG into their rating practices.

The tone of the conversation fluctuates wildly between the three reports, and this was the basis for my criticism as I cited earlier. The first two reports cede far too much room to the credit rating agencies, and their line of argument that protects them most. Interestingly, the investors base was insistent and consistent with its requirements; develop better signposts for what the rating agencies are doing, and transmit it better. They also developed what I would consider to be the correct narrative in that credit rating agencies have a much larger role to play in the development of the concept of sustainable investment than they are currently taking. There is likely many reasons as to why they would not—it may impact upon their relationships with issuers who are their main source of revenue, it may open them up to more liability then they are comfortable with, or they may genuinely refuse to accept that it is their role—but the final understanding is a clear one from the interactions between investors and the credit rating agencies; 'do more'.

The question then becomes whether the credit rating agencies will rise to the challenges or rely upon the oligopolistic protection to continue partially investing in the concept of sustainable business, if we believe that to be the case. Also, what factors may impact upon which outcome prevails? How does the market structure within the credit rating industry affect which outcome prevails? Fascinatingly, the intricacies in this regard are developing all the time, so it is certainly worth examining where the credit rating agencies are up to with responding to these requests from the investor base.

4.2.2 *S&P's Reaction to the Investor Base*

S&P were early leaders in terms of engaging with the ESG issue. This is not surprising given that S&P leads the oligopoly by way of market share, and their early endeavours involved producing research and, essentially, their organisational stance on specific ESG issues. One report to note in particular was their *Climate Risk: Rising Tides Raise the Stakes* report published in 2015, which involved a number of different perspectives from within the organisation on the 'E' variant of ESG.[47] However, whilst such reports are useful and interesting, the investor base has been clear as to what it wants, and this report unfortunately does not cut it. But, the Climate-related report was an early outlier so it can be excused for not getting to the point. Now, particularly since the integration into the PRI, there is no such excuse; S&P know what is required. In 2019, they published *The Role of Environmental, Social, and Governance Credit Factors in our Ratings Analysis*, which available via their website represents their most up-to-date account of how they integrate ESG into their rating actions, as per the investors' request.[48]

S&P start by detailing example ESG drivers of rating actions. These include such factors as greenhouse gas emissions, health and safety violations, and internal control factors, amongst a large list of others. This frames what S&P understand to be potentially material factors, which is then accentuated by examples of previous rating actions which have been impacted by ESG issues which, helpfully, range from 'E', 'S', and 'G' examples. The majority of examples cited involve rating downgrades of different sorts, although there are examples of ESG factors contributing to rating upgrades, which illustrates the points advanced during the roundtable sessions with the PRI.

Nevertheless, the investor base want concrete information on how ESG is integrated into the credit rating process. What they receive from S&P will probably not be entirely satisfying. The agency start by declaring that materiality and effect differs from industry to industry, and then between participants within those industries. This is followed by yet another warning, this time in the shape of declaring that the influence of ESG on credit ratings change over time, and the further into the future the ESG factor may impact a rating, the less accurate it becomes and the less it is considered. This is the finally followed by the declaration that international disclosure-related standards and regulations would improve the content and accuracy of ESG-related credit rating actions, which points towards a lack of useful information available, rather than any internal problems with the agencies (which may well be the case).

But, S&P do start providing details. They detail how ESG credit factors are considered and integrated by sector. However, the word 'may' is consistently used, leading to an understanding that the subjectivity in S&P's integration of ESG is going nowhere anytime soon. For example, with regard to their processes for analysing corporates, S&P say that:

> For example, if we consider that emerging or increasing environmental or social risks will cause industry-specific growth trends to deteriorate, or the level and trend of industry profit margins to weaken, we may revise down our assessment of industry risk for that industry. This, in turn, would weigh on the business risk profiles of rated obligors in that industry.[49]

What is missing from the document is any indication as to what may need to be witnessed in order for S&P to consider that 'E' or 'S' risks are having a greater impact. Also, how do we know *how likely* they are to revise down their assessment? At what point in the process will this happen? If it would, in turn, weigh on the business risk profiles of rated obligors in the affected industry, then to what degree? When would that weight be conveyed to the industry, and in what manner would that reflect on the credit ratings? There are too many questions emanating from a document designed to make the process clearer. This, unfortunately, is repeated across all of the different sectors cited in the document.

Interestingly, the only aspect that has clearer details of the process is the process for rating sovereign entities on account of ESG factors. This is because of the different in factor, presumably. Although, in other areas, the agency is not as forthcoming with information regarding impact. With regard to structured finance, the agency is somewhat dismissive of the impact of ESG; the agency declares immediately that 'we generally do not anticipate ESG credit factors to be key rating drivers in this sector'. The reason for this, S&P claim, is because there is likely legal protection within the structured product that somewhat mitigates the effects of ESG factors; the example cited is the minimal impact of a swathe of hurricanes in 2017 on US Residential Mortgage-Backed Securities, because of the geographical variance built into the product. That makes complete sense. There are likely similar arguments that would be brought forward for other sectors, but a good example of massive ESG impacts across the spectrum of a section could be the Commercial Mortgage-Backed Securities market, which is undergoing particular stress because of the pandemic (and before).[50]

Interestingly, that is it. That is all that is available from S&P on how they integrate ESG into the ratings. Nothing concrete, no examples of to what extent ESG is considered, how likely it may be that ESG is considered. Does this meet what the investors asked for? It is doubtful. It is questionable, actually, what an investor would have gotten from reading the document that they would not have gotten from, say, any of the PRI reports.

4.2.3 Moody's Reaction to the Investor Base

Moody's, like S&P, had published a number of documents over the past few years detailing their views on ESG integration. Unfortunately, some previous versions have been locked behind pay-walls (although they are now available freely)[51] which is far from progressive, but their most recent version, entitled *General Principles for Assessing Environmental, Social, and Governance Risks* was published in 2019[52] and then amended in late 2020.[53] The first warning sign is the inclusion of the terms 'general' and 'principles' which indicate particular detail will be lacking.

There is, like S&P, many instances of the word 'may' being utilised. There are also many instances of Moody's echoing the S&P report by providing vague instances of when certain methodological actions *may* occur. There are also a number of instances where the common responses to criticisms are provided, like ESG is difficult to define and thus difficult to opine on, or the lack of internationally agreed upon standards for ESG disclosure hurt the rating process. For the record, it is not that these observations are untrue. Irrespective of criticism that is rightly levelled at the credit rating agencies, a lot of these points are valid. What is not valid is refusing to cede to the wishes of the market because one's product is central to the functioning of the market. However, there are signs that this is changing. S&P's most recent report according to their website was from 2019, as was Moody's' offering. Fitch, as we shall see next, have a more recent offering that clearly indicates that the lessons from the PRI initiative, at least, are being acted upon. Fortunately, as this chapter was being written, Moody's updated their methodological disclosure at the end of 2020 and it includes a sea-change in their approach, arguably.

Their document contains everything that S&P's does: general principles for rating ESG; warnings over the limitations that come with rating ESG factors; the individuality to sectors that makes wider ESG ratings difficult. These are common elements to these documents because, for the credit rating agencies, it is important to articulate them for investors/consumers. However, in the 2019 version, that is all there was. On reflection, it was rather limited and certainly not befitting of one of the first entities to join the credit risk initiative with the PRI. In the 2020 version, there is something different as soon as you start reading:

> We have introduced three distinct E, S and G issuer profile scores (IPSs) that indicate our opinion of the extent to which a given issuer or transaction is exposed to E, S and G risks (incorporating ESG-specific mitigants) or benefits from its exposure to E, S or G. We have also introduced an overall ESG Credit Impact Score (CIS), which is a qualitative assessment of how ESG considerations impact the rating of an issuer or transaction. We have provided additional detail on the quantitative and qualitative considerations informing our assessments of the IPSs for sovereigns, and how we establish CISs in that sector. IPSs and CISs will be established for issuers and transactions over time.[54]

These scores are Moody's' attempts to cater the claim that they are not telling the market how they are integrating ESG into their rating processes, and to what extend when they do. The Issuer Profile Scores are part of the agency's cross-sector methodology, but interestingly their 'ESG Credit Impact Score' has its own rating scale of:

- CIS-1 > Positive
- CIS-2 > Neutral-to-low
- CIS-3 > Moderately Negative
- CIS-4 > Highly Negative
- CIS-5 > Very Highly Negative.

As Moody's say themselves in the report, 'The ESG credit impact score is an output of the rating process that more transparently communicates the impact of ESG considerations on the rating of an issuer or transaction'.

The Issuer Profile Scores help to feed ESG into the credit rating process, and 'illustrate the issuer's exposure' to ESG risks. It also incorporates any mitigating factors, or benefits, that may have an influence on the credit profile of the target. Moody's are consistent in their messaging that an Issuer Profile Score is not the foundation of rating actions, but a contributing factor; to provide context, Moody's state that two issuers may have exactly the same credit rating but very different IPSs. Furthermore, an issuer may be exposed to larger ESG-related risks, but may have either a strong structure that mitigates the damage potentially caused, or has other credit-related strengths that positively affect its creditworthiness. The IPSs are expressed on a 5-point scale, from E-1, S-1, or G-1 (positive) to E-5, S-5, or G-5 (very highly negative). If there is missing data, which is an issue when there are no disclosure standards, Moody's will rely on sector-based data to assume the impact on the issuer, relative to their peers.

With regard to the Credit Impact Score (CIS), the usual caveats are offered. The process is inherently qualitative because of the difficulty of isolating the particular impacts of ESG and non-ESG factors. Also, like IPSs, there is no direct correlation between a CIS and an issuer's credit rating. It is only at the extremes does the CIS potentially relate to the credit rating, i.e. a CIS of CIS-5 would indicate that the issuer is particularly and negatively impacted by ESG issues, which would have had an impact in the issuer receiving a lowly credit rating. The sentiment is that one will not see a AAA rating attached to a CIS-5 rating, theoretically speaking (although it is possible because mitigating factors may negate the negative impact of the CIS score).

It likely looks like a small amendment with not much changing. But, this is a massive change for Moody's. There are enough caveats in the report to indicate that this is still an extraordinarily liability-averse organisation, but the addition of the CIS directly responds to investors' requests. That in itself, irrespective of the impact that the CIS addition will have, tells us a lot. Yet, they were not the first to make this move.

4.2.4 *Fitch Ratings' Reaction to the Investor Base*

Before 2019, Fitch were almost dismissive of the concept of integrating and then articulating the impact of ESG. They were not, of course, but the feeling compared to the two market leaders was very different. Writing now, it is arguably the case that this was because they were developing something that would enhance the credit rating proposition, rather than talking about it. In 2019, and directly because of the PRI and the vocalisation of the investor base, Fitch launched its 'ESG Relevance Scores'.

This was the first time anybody in the credit rating arena had done so, and was then described in detail within Fitch's most recent report on the issue, entitled *ESG in Credit: White Paper*.[55]

Interestingly, Fitch want to contextualise the development of their ESG Relevance Scores product, and detail for us the importance of connecting with investors via the PRI:

> Transparency regarding the influence of ESG issues on credit ratings has also concerned investors, as highlighted by PRI's Statement on ESG in credit risk and ratings. As signatories to the statement and in keeping with our core values, the Fitch Ratings' ESG Relevance Scores were developed to assist investors with their credit analysis and to provide transparency around the material ESG issues that have influenced Fitch's credit ratings.
>
> Fitch spent several months gathering the views and opinions of a range of market stakeholders on what they wanted credit rating agencies to provide before devising our relevance scores. The investor-based UN PRI's CRA initiative was also instrumental in vocalizing what investors want from CRAs: public disclosure of ESG credit issues at an industry and sector level, and transparent descriptions of how ESG issues affect individual company credit ratings, as well as identification of systemic ESG risks. While investors can access many and varied data sources when seeking to manage portfolios in a more sustainable manner, nothing specifically highlighted entity- and sector-level ESG risk elements for fundamental credit risk.[56]

Whereas Moody's' rating scale for their CIS framework applies extremes, the Fitch model has a linear scale. It spans from 1 to 5, and an ESG Relevance Score of 5 indicates that the given factor, on a stand-alone basis, has a direct impact on the rating. A score of 1 indicates no impact at all (or at least negligible). If the factor affects the entity positively, a '+' signifier will be placed against the Relevance Score to indicate this. It is also interesting to note that the same analysts developing the credit rating will be the ones developing the ESG Relevance Score for the same entity, which only further increases the authority of the Relevance Scores.

When a score of 4 or 5 is presented, the result is that the issue will become a point of discussion for the relevant rating committee. For the final rating, the final score will be published, as will information in its 'reference' box; this highlights the areas in the rating where ESG issues are captured. To formulate the Score, Fitch utilises publicly available information, as well as engagement with the entity's management. They also utilise peer information, regulatory information, and sector analysis.

According to Fitch, they have applied the Relevance Scores to a host of issuances since launching the addition, although some sectors have not had the addition applied, like CDOs.

Fitch have made up for what seemed to be a sluggish start to their integration of the concept of ESG, and also the articulation of how they consider it. However, in their defence, waiting to see the outcomes of newly-developed areas of dialogue with investors bore fruit, and their new addition will surely become an industry standard moving forward. Their articulation of their model, and also their understanding of ESG and its importance moving forward, is impressive.

4.3 The Credit Rating Agencies Continue to Move Forward

Whilst S&P have not detailed a similar approach to Fitch and Moody's, it will only be a matter of time; experience tells us that very few innovations within an oligopoly stay exclusive for long. There are, of course, different factors affecting each of the members of the oligopoly. For Fitch, getting ahead of the game can have huge benefits in establishing themselves as a true partner of the mainstream. For S&P, as the market leader, getting it right is more important, rather than being the first mover.

What is interesting to note is that all three agencies make it abundantly clear that they are not opining on the ESG strategies of the entities they are rating. What their approaches merely detail is that credit rating agencies *do* integrate ESG into their rating considerations, and now they are detailing *how*. This is useful for investors. It is useful to know if a highly-rated company may have ESG factors affecting their future rates of growth, etc. The actual dissemination of this new addition is particularly clean and integrated clearly within the rating action (particularly in the case of Fitch).

However, what would it take for the agencies to start making those assessments? They now have a suitable vehicle within which they could include such assessments and would only really need the underlying assessment which could be acquired from absorbing existing CSSs, or developing their own ESG analytical models. What is key for this chapter is to recognise that the credit rating agencies understand the importance of reacting positively to the demands of the market. Some of the narrative throughout the PRI's development could be construed as stubborn, in their refusal to cede any potential liability. This is commonly represented throughout the agencies' history and is central to their culture; whilst this is of true of every private entity of course, it is *particularly* true of the credit rating industry. In providing even more opinion on ESG-related concerns and lifting the curtain on how ESG is integrated, the agencies are, theoretically at least, opening themselves up to more scrutiny. They do not like that. However, the rewards are worth the risk, and the agencies have demonstrated that they understand this. S&P will follow suit.

The rating dynamic has progressed as a result. The market has continued to the use the credit rating agencies since the Financial Crisis just as much, if not more than they used to. They are now detailing how the agencies should serve their needs as the mainstream moves towards labelling itself as 'sustainable', via the integration of ESG into its culture. The credit rating agencies have all of the necessary components to fulfil this role, and all the parties in the dynamic know it: rating agencies, investors, and issuers. What we are likely to see is regulators join that list shortly, in *reacting* to the market dynamic. That will be covered more in the final chapter, but for us it is important to understand this dynamic is greater detail. Analysing this dynamic and the factors that affect it allow us to understand better what has happened, why certain actions are being taken, and what may happen next.

Notes

1. James Fontanella-Khan, Ortenca Aliaj, and Harry Dempsey, 'S&P Global to Buy ISH Markit in $44bn deal' (2020) *Financial Times* (Nov 30). https://www.ft.com/content/fb040ea4-868d-4491-8c13-8169b97255d5 (accessed 15 December 2020).
2. Marc Flandreau, Norbet Gaillard, and Frank Packer, 'To Err Is Human: US Rating Agencies and the Interwar Foreign Government Debt Crisis' (2011) 15 *European Review of Economic History* 495–538; Marc Flandreau and Joanna K. Sławatyniec, 'Understanding Rating Addiction: US Courts and the Origins of Rating Agencies' Regulatory Licence (1900–1940)' (2013) 20 *Financial History Review* 3 237–257; Marc Flandreau and Gabriel G. Mesevage, 'The Separation of Information and Lending and the Rise of the Rating Agencies in the USA (1841–1907)' (2014) 62 *Scandinavian Economic History Review* 3 213–242; Marc Flandreau and Gabriel G. Mesevage, 'The Untold History of Transparency: Mercantile

Agencies, the Law, and the Lawyers (1851–1916)' (2014) 15 *Enterprise and Society* 2 213–251.

3. Richard Sylla 'An Historical Primer on the Business of Credit Ratings' in Richard M. Levich, Giovanni Majnoni, and Carmen Reinhart, *Ratings, Rating Agencies, and the Global Financial System* (Kluwer 2002); Herwig P. Langohr and Patricia T Langohr, *The Rating Agencies and Their Credit Ratings: What They Are, How They Work, and Why They Are Relevant* (John Wiley & Sons 2010); Daniel Cash, *Regulation and the Credit Rating Agencies: Restraining Ancillary Services* (Routledge 2018) Chapter 1.
4. Pilar Abad, Rodrigo Ferraras, and M-Delores Robles, 'Informational Role of Rating Revisions After Reputational Events and Regulation Reforms' (2019) 62 *International Review of Financial Analysis* 91, 92.
5. Frank Partnoy, 'What's (Still) Wrong with Credit Ratings' (2017) 92 *Washington Law Review* 1407, 1424.
6. Daniel Cash, 'Credit Rating Agency Regulation Since the Financial Crisis: The Evolution of the "Regulatory Licence" Concept' in Daniel Cash and Robert Goddard (eds) *Regulation and the Global Financial Crisis: Impact, Regulatory Responses, and Beyond* (Routledge 2020).
7. Joseph W. Errant, *Law Relating to Mercantile Agencies* (1889 T & J.W. Johnson & Co) 1; Rowena Olegario, *The Engine of Enterprise: Credit in America* (Harvard University Press 2016) 229.
8. Marc Flandreau and Gabriel G. Mesevage, 'The Separation of Information and Lending and the Rise of the Rating Agencies in the USA (1841–1907)' (2014) 62 *Scandinavian Economic History Review* 3 229.
9. Ralph Hidy, 'Credit Rating Before Dun and Bradstreet' (1939) 13 *Bulletin of the Business Historical* 6.
10. Ibid., 88.
11. Olegario (n 7) 64.
12. Edward J. Balleisen, 'Vulture Capitalism in Antebellum America: The 1841 Federal Bankruptcy Act and the Exploitation of Financial Distress' (1996) 70 *The Business History Review* 4 495.
13. For more on this sequence of events see Marc Flandreau and Gabriel G. Mesevage, 'The Separation of Information and Lending and the Rise of the Rating Agencies in the USA (1841–1907)' (2014) 62 *Scandinavian Economic History Review* 3 230; and Marc Flandreau and Gabriel G Mesevage, 'The Untold History of Transparency: Mercantile Agencies, the Law, and the Lawyers (1851–1916)' (2014) 15 *Enterprise and Society* 2 220.
14. For more on the fascinating Lewis Tappan, His Agency, and its Development, see: Bertram Wyatt-Brown, 'God and Dun and Bradstreet, 1841–1851' (1966) 40 *The Business History Review* 4; Scott Sandage,

Born Losers: A History of Failure in America (Harvard University Press 2006).
15. Richard S. Wilson and Frank J. Fabozzi, *Corporate Bonds: Structures and Analysis* (Frank J Fabozzi Associates 1996) 210.
16. Marta Poon, 'Rating Agencies' in Karin K. Cetina and Alex Prada, *The Oxford Handbook of the Sociology of Finance* (Oxford University Press 2012) 276.
17. John Moody, *Moody's Manual of Industrial and Miscellaneous Securities* (The O.C. Lewis Company 1900).
18. (n 15) 211.
19. Daniel Cash, 'Scope Ratings: The Viability of a Response' (2018) 15 *European Company Law* 1, 6–10.
20. Andrew Fight, *Understanding International Bank Risk* (John Wiley & Sons 2004) 48.
21. Mary Buffett and David Clark, *Warren Buffett and the Art of Stock Arbitrage: Proven Strategies for Arbitrage and Other Special Investment Situations* (Simon and Schuster 2010) 122.
22. *The Credit Rating Agency Duopoly Relief Act of 2005* H.R. 2990; *The Credit Rating Agency Reform Act of 2006* Pub. L. 109–291, 120 Stat. 1327.
23. Mark Zandi, *Financial Shock: Global Panic and Government Bailouts—How We Got Here and What Must Be Done to Fix It* (FT Press 2009) 117.
24. Eric Tymoigne and Larry Wray, *The Rise and Fall of Money Manager Capitalism: Minsky's Half Century from World War Two to the Great Recession* (Routledge 2013) 142.
25. See Daniel Cash, *Regulation and the Credit Rating Agencies: Restraining Ancillary Services* (Routledge 2018) Chapter 2.
26. *The Dodd-Frank Wall Street Reform and Consumer Protection Act of 2010* Pub.L. 111–203, H.R. 4173.
27. Regulation (EU) No 1060/2009 [2009] OJ L302/1; Regulation (EU) No 513/2011 [2011] OJ L145/30; Regulation (EU) No 462/2013 [2013] OJ L146/1.
28. US Department of Justice, 'Remarks for Attorney General Eric Holder Press Conference Announcing Settlement with S&P' (2015). https://www.justice.gov/opa/speech/remarks-attorney-general-eric-holder-press-conference-announcing-settlement-sp (accessed 19 December 2020).
29. Niccolo Nirino, Gabriele Santoro, Nicola Miglietta, and Robert Quaglia, 'Corporate Controversies and Company's Financial Performance: Exploring the Moderating role of ESG Practices' (2021) 162 *Technological Forecasting & Social Change* 120, 341, 2.
30. Mikael Petitjean, 'Eco-friendly Policies and Financial Performance: Was the Financial Crisis a Game Changer for Large US Companies?' (2019) 80 *Energy Economics* 502–511.

31. Diane-Laure Arjaliés, Philip Grant, Iain Hardie, Donald MacKenzie, and Ekaterina Svetlova, *Chains of Finance: How Investment Management is Shaped* (OUP 2017) 129.
32. Stefan Leins, '"Responsible Investment": ESG and the post-Crisis Ethical Order' (2020) 49 *Economy and Society* 1 71–91, 72.
33. Florian Kiesel and Felix Lücke, 'ESG in Credit Ratings and the Impact on Financial Markets' (2019) 28 *Financial Markets Institutions and Instruments* 263–290, 277.
34. Ruoke Yang, 'Credit Rating in the Age of Environmental, Social, and Governance (ESG)' (2020) SSRN. https://papers.ssrn.com/sol3/papers.cfm?abstract_id=3595376, 16.
35. PRI, *Credit Risk and Ratings Initiative* (2020) https://www.unpri.org/investment-tools/fixed-income/credit-risk-and-ratings.
36. Daniel Cash, *The Role of Credit Rating Agencies in Responsible Finance* (Palgrave Macmillan 2018).
37. Neil S. Eccles, 'UN Principles for Responsible Investment Signatories and the Anti-Apartheid SRI Movement: A Thought Experiment' [2010] 95 *Journal of Business Ethics* 415–424, 416.
38. Ibid., 423.
39. Sakis Kotsantonis, Chris Pinney, and George Serafeim, 'ESG Integration in Investment Management: Myths and Realities' [2016] 28 *Journal of Applied Corporate Finance* 2 10–17, 12.
40. Arleta A.A. Majoch, Andreas G.F. Hoepner, and Tessa Hebb, 'Sources of Stakeholder Salience in the Responsible Investment Movement: Why Do Investors Sign the Principles for Responsible Investment?' [2017] 140 *Journal of Business Ethics* 723–741, 723.
41. Ibid., 724.
42. The Principles for Responsible Investment, *Shifting Perceptions: ESG, Credit Risk and Ratings—Part 1: The State of Play* (2017). https://www.unpri.org/download?ac=256 (accessed 22 December 2020) 9.
43. Ibid., 17.
44. The Principles for Responsible Investment, *Shifting Perceptions: ESG, Credit Risk and Ratings—Part 2: Exploring the Disconnects* (2018) https://www.unpri.org/download?ac=4813 (accessed 23 December 2020) 7.
45. The Principles for Responsible Investment, *Shifting Perceptions: ESG, Credit Risk and Ratings—Part 3: From Disconnects to Action Areas* (2018). https://www.unpri.org/download?ac=5819 (accessed 23 December 2020) 10.
46. Ibid.
47. Standard & Poor's, *Insights—Climate Risk: Rising Tides Raise the Stakes* (2015). https://www.spratings.com/documents/20184/984172/Ins

ights+Magazine+-+December+2015/cff352af-4f50-4f15-a765-f56dcd4ee5c8 (accessed 23 December 2020).

48. S&P, *The Role of Environmental, Social, and Governance Credit Factors in our Ratings Analysis* (2019). https://www.spglobal.com/ratings/en/research/articles/190912-the-role-of-environmental-social-and-governance-credit-factors-in-our-ratings-analysis-11135920 (accessed 23 December 2020).
49. Ibid.
50. For information on the issues built into the CMBS market and associated issues with ratings, see generally H. Kent Baker, Greg Filbeck, and Andrew C. Spieler, *Debt Markets and Investments* (Oxford University Press 2019); for more information on the CMBS market in particular and the problems affecting it, see Sumit Agarwal, Brent W. Ambrose, Luis A. Lopez, and Xue Xiao, 'Pandemic Risk Factors and the Role of Government Intervention: Evidence from COVID-19 and CMBS Mortgage Performance' (2020) SSRN. https://papers.ssrn.com/sol3/papers.cfm?abstract_id=3674960 (accessed 23 December 2020).
51. Moody's 'Environmental, Social and Governance (ESG) Global: Moody's Approach to Assessing ESG in Credit Analysis' (2018). https://www.moodys.com/researchdocumentcontentpage.aspx?docid=PBC_1089067 (accessed 23 December 2020).
52. Moody's, *General Principles for Assessing Environmental, Social and Governance Risks* (Moody's 2019). https://www.moodys.com/researchdocumentcontentpage.aspx?docid=PBC_1133569 (accessed 23 December 2020).
53. Moody's, *General Principles for Assessing Environmental, Social and Governance Risks* (Moody's 2020). https://www.moodys.com/researchdocumentcontentpage.aspx?docid=PBC_1243406 (accessed 23 December 2020).
54. Ibid., 2.
55. Fitch Ratings, *ESG in Credit: White Paper* (2020). https://downloads.ctfassets.net/03fbs7oah13w/3ML3lNLlWrtW3KJsdSx7AV/fec2197a6e56ba4a042e14a96d445fb2/esg-2020-english.pdf?mkt_tok=eyJpIjoiTVdVNU5UQTVZekEwWkRjMCIsInQiOiI3OTdvcUNONmRWaVErckoxcUloQThTNVwveW02b2p2XC9tSWZcL05RRGdpK1FjUEhmSXFQY2l6VzYxbFpuU1lwV1c4VlMwTkpcL3JOSWJWNWI3MnlPeHRPWHVTczVhM3FQcVZaOTB1UnJiekVNVVwvdjRGbHJ1R3Q4T0w2NXppWE41MEg5ODduTWFhM1hRUTZXNDQ2RWVFTGZJZz09In0%3D (accessed 24 December 2020).
56. Ibid., 6.

CHAPTER 5

'An Undercurrent of Need': Understanding the Dynamics of the Responsible Rating Relationship

Just like in the credit rating arena, the sustainability rating arena is defined by the dynamics at play within it. All of the parties concerned have different needs and expect different outcomes. However, for the continuation of the 'mainstreamisation' of the concept of sustainable investing, the investor base needs certain things in particular. The aim of this book is to ascertain whether the CSS universe, or the credit rating industry can best serve that particular need. Yet, there are a number of nuanced elements that we need to further understand to better ascertain the answer to that question.

In the credit rating world, sector-defining regulations implemented in the wake of the Financial Crisis have, for the most part, failed. In the CSS arena, there are no regulations in place yet, but the CSSs are widely being criticised for not meeting the needs of the mainstream investors, as we have seen. I have argued consistently that the reason for regulatory inefficiency in this market is simply down to a misunderstanding of the underlying dynamics of the *role* of rating agencies. That misunderstanding could be because of a number of reasons—either by lack of information, a consequence of the 'revolving door' theory, or something else entirely—but the reasons are merely something to discuss and debate; the result is the same. Regulatory inefficiency is often cited as one of the major causes of disfunction in the rating arena, but the reality may be that regulators *cannot* efficiently act in this arena because of the underlying dynamics.

D. Cash, *Sustainability Rating Agencies vs Credit Rating Agencies*, Palgrave Studies in Impact Finance,
https://doi.org/10.1007/978-3-030-71693-6_5

There are a number of angles to examine. But, if we are to continue with our analysis, we need to understand a few elements much better. The first is to consider who the 'investor' is, and what they want. The identity of what the 'investor' has changed massively in a relatively short space of time, and what they need has changed also. By understanding who they are, and then how this relates to their needs, we can better understand who may be better placed to serve them. Once we understand the investor better, then what they need will become clearer. We will assess what they need, and this will feed into the perfect model that can deliver that need. This revelation will lead us into the final chapter that will detail which industry may be the best suited to serve the mainstream investor in their apparent quest to integrate ESG concerns into the investment strategies.

5.1 Institutional Investor Supremacy

Particularly in American economic history, the trajectory of what an 'investor' was has changed dramatically. Traditionally, so-called retail investors owned the majority of public stock in the marketplace. This came with a number of associated benefits and drawbacks. Given that the U.S. has a particular economic culture, stock ownership formed the foundation of a culture that is particularly aligned to the concept of the free market. Yet, there were a number of drawbacks, and the largest failing of the American marketplace before the Financial Crisis—the stock market crash of 1929 and the ensuing Great Depression—was all founded on the exuberance, and subsequent exploitation of the 'retail investor'.[1] Perhaps one of the most significant legislative responses in U.S. history—the 'New Deal' of the 1930s—supports the argument that the retail investor was considered to be the cornerstone of the American economy and needed to be protected.[2]

The opposite of a retail investor is an institutional investor, who are also known as a 'sophisticated investor'. This label explains the view of the retail investor at the same time, positioning them as an 'unsophisticated investor'. The result of this is that their position is considered to be one of lacking necessary information, which when combined with a lack of skill needed to understand complicated financial products, means they need particular things from the market and its intermediaries. For example, a retail investor may need increased levels of disclosure from issuers, and/or simplified analysis from intermediaries like credit rating agencies, so that they can understand the underlying fundamentals of the investment opportunity in front of them. Also, they will need this information and substitution for their lack of skill to be affordable enough to justify the investment. It is for these reasons, and the incredible acceleration in systemic complexity over the past four or five decades that has resulted in the supremacy of the retail investor being 'deader than disco'.[3] Coffee explains that 'today, retail investors account for only a modest minority of the ownership of large, publicly traded companies and probably only between 2 and 4% of the trading in NYSE-listed companies'. He suggests that 'retail investors seem to have finally realised that they are poor stock pickers who systematically lose money when they trade actively on their own. As a result, they have migrated in large numbers to invest in highly diversified institutional intermediaries'.[4]

These 'institutional intermediaries' Coffee talks of are some of, if not the biggest private entities in the world. He talks specifically about the 'Big Three'—note the theme of concentration being the market's preference in a variety of arenas—institutional investors: BlackRock, State Street, and Vanguard. These are not the only players, but are massive factors when it comes to private investment bodies. There are also massive pension funds, mutual funds, and sovereign bodies that make up the modern-day investment landscape. As Coffee rightly noted, these entities are incredibly diversified in their holdings, which has led to them being labelled as 'Universal Owners':

> Universal owners have been defined as large investors who hold a range of investments in different listed companies as well as other assets and are therefore tied to the performance of markets of whole economies, rather than the performance of individual assets.[5]

When the word 'investor' has been used in this book, this is who we are referring to. These entities control more assets than a lot of countries or regions hold. The theory of 'universal ownership' is one that has been applied to the industry, and one that it has adopted openly. There are some issues with the theory, but it is of interest. Quigley discusses how the Universal Owners have an interest in the economy as a whole due to its widely diversified holdings and 'cannot reasonably sell out of individual companies whose activities add costs to the balance sheets of other companies in its portfolio'. This foundational element to the theory brings forth an array of subsequent issues and nuances. For example, the fact that divesting from one company could negatively impact on another company the investor has a large stake in means that there must be a longer-term focus applied by the investor's management team, in theory. Quigley talks about how this encourages the principle of intergenerational justice, in that the fiduciary duties of the institutional investor's management team means that the impact on others, and on future generations, must be considered.[6] This is also why Solomon argues that institutional investors are so interested in ESG integration, as it complements their longer-term perspectives.[7] Robins also notes that, inherently, institutional investors have an incentive to reduce negative externalities in their portfolios, which also provides reason for the interest in integrating ESG into their processes.[8] Coincidentally, it has been suggested in the literature that retail investors do not generally share this interest, because of the different time-horizons that they tend to apply.[9]

Hawley and Williams noted the rapid acceleration of institutional stock ownership in the U.S. even at the turn of the century,[10] with it being suggested recently that the 'Big Three' manage more than $15 trillion in global assets, control almost 80% of the exchange-traded fund market, and over the past decade have attracted more than 80% of *all* investor money in the U.S.[11] It is different in different regions of course, with the E.U. having a very different investment landscape, China being predominantly controlled by the Chinese State apparatus, and other regions making for a very varied landscape for institutionalised investment (some regions are dominated by sovereign wealth funds, i.e. the Middle East, whilst some are geographically separated i.e. the Oceanic region). The E.U. is a particularly good example of the diversity of investing culture, because with its multi-State bloc consisting of culturally different entities, a combined investment culture is hard to cultivate; de Haan et al. note how the E.U. has stronger Western entities, lower-investing entities in the South, and less developed investing entities in the East.[12]

This is why it is tremendously important to understand, as Coffee says, that 'one size does not fit all'. Not all institutional investors are the same. They range in their formulation, and therefore their ambitions, strategies, and internal processes are all varied. It has been suggested that the differences can be witnessed in their aims relative to the market:

> Not all institutional investors are alike. Some mutual funds and many hedge funds are "stock pickers"; they engage in active trading, and believe they can outperform the efficient market. Generally, they are wrong, but not invariably (which could be explained by the fact that some may have access

> to private information). Still, a larger percentage of institutional investors are diversified (or even indexed) than are individual investors, and typically these highly diversified investors do not attempt to outperform the market (but rather to mirror it cheaply).[13]

This aim has a direct impact upon the strategy of most institutional investors. For example, it makes sense that the institutional investor has different requirements than an individual investor, and that comes in a variety of forms. An institutional investor will not necessarily want their companies diversifying any more than is necessary, because the act of diversifying to spread risk is already done within the wide portfolio, whereas for the individual investor wants the company to diversify to help spread their own risk as an investor. This divergence is also reflected in the need for more information than an individual investor would ever want, and in a particular format also:

> The inference best drawn from this evidence is that diversified institutional investors want at least as much information (and probably more) as do individual investors, and they want a standardised format to enhance the comparability of disclosures across companies. Particularly as they come to make decisions on a portfolio-wide basis, diversified institutions will increasingly want to know and compare the gains and losses at multiple firms in their portfolio that will result from voting decisions that they may make. In contrast, undiversified shareholders have no such need to make similar comparisons.[14]

It is no coincidence that one of the most consistent requests from investors partnered with the PRI, as we saw in Chapter 3, is for the information to be standardised and therefore comparable.

The investor base has a varied existence. However, the increasing authority of the largest investors, as they continue to become more concentrated, is having a particular effect upon the issuers, and the informational intermediaries. It has been noted that 20% of the S&P500 is held by the Big Three, and that they have even larger voting powers. This is increasingly giving the institutional investors a 'voice' that they are being encouraged to use and, if and when they join forces (as they sometimes do), their voice is not only considerable, but significant.[15] Coffee suggests that this role is actually more impactful in practice, as company managers will be personally risk-averse and unwilling to jeopardise their own careers in fighting these massive financial entities. This sentiment underpins the American culture, and although we will look at this issue in much more detail in the next chapter, it is worth noting that the American State apparatus have actively refused to regulate and legislate on areas such as non-financial disclosure, instead preferring to let the institutional investors dictate the will of the market via their activism. However, despite the support given to this cultural approach—which is not shared in other regions like the E.U., as we shall see in the next chapter—there are massive issues with it. Monks and Minnow describe how, in reality, only a handful of the large entities, including private and public organisations ranging from organisations like BlackRock, to pension funds like CalPERS, have been active in terms of voting for change; as the authors state:

> It is important to note that of the very large group of public plans, only a handful have been actively involved in governance initiatives. One of these activists noted, There might be lots of noise and action, and there might be talk about all the new, awakened shareholders and institutional investors, but there's really not much more than a dozen public pension funds involved. And they call the tune. In fact if you took the CalPERS and the New York City pension fund and TIAA–CREF out of the equation along with our fund [New York State] and Wisconsin, Pennsylvania and to some extent Florida, you might have very little activism at all.[16]

The authors subsequently raise valid points: Who can govern such entities? Are the trustees truly accountable? How can inevitable conflicts of interests be managed and minimised? Essentially, what the US culture has produced is governance by private bodies. Quigley, relying on the views of Elinor Ostrom, Hawley, and Urwin, wonders whether institutional investors (a) know that they should, (b) have the capacity to, and (c) can do so even with the help of the government, *govern*. She muses whether, in reality, the concept of a universal owner is an academic one, applied to an unwilling industry.[17] It may be good to write on a website, but truly becoming a universal owner and taking on board that role is a particularly difficult task; one wonders whether this is why the progress of true ESG integration has been slow, or at least not as fast as it could have been.

Whilst some believe that the changing in investing supremacy can and will change the concept of 'shareholder value',[18] the important understanding for us is that the institutional investor requires certain things with respect to their position. Complete and comparable information is required from providers that can be trusted, and who do not create duplicative costs. We can see now that the 'mainstreamisation' of the concept of ESG is of systemic importance, but there are particular elements that must be addressed; the first is that information needs to be standardised.

5.2 The Need for Standardisationn

When we talk of standardisation in relation to ESG, we are really talking about two particular elements. The first is the information that is sent out into the arena by issuers, and the second is the information that is sent out by the CSSs and, to a growing extent, the credit rating agencies. Now that we understand that the 'investors' are, for the most part, institutional investors who will likely hold a highly diversified portfolio of investments, the need to compare the ESG-related performance of investable opportunities, or of those companies one is already invested in, is clearly important.

This has been well documented. It is also one of the most forthcoming arguments from investors when asked what may be the largest hurdles for the progression of the mainstreamisation of ESG integration; Ted Eliopoulous, Chief Investment Officer for CalPERS, said at a SASB-organised symposium that 'what we've been finding is that our managers take a wide variety of approaches. But the one common theme we hear in the responses of both our internal and external managers is the need for much more standardised information and data'.[19] Others have found the same issue, with Amel-Zadeh and Serafeim confirming that 'a lack of standardisation and quantification are the main obstacles to ESG integration', with a 'lack of comparability of reported information across firms' also being cited.[20] Another reason why it is so important for institutional investors is because being able to compare such information allows them to predict, even more so, the potential impact of one action—say a particular vote—on other entities within the portfolio, etc.[21]

On the side of information disclosed from issuers, there is no agreed-upon standard for disclosing data. Unlike financial reporting, non-financial reporting is currently undertaken on a voluntary basis. To jump ahead for a moment into the analysis in the next chapter, the U.S. and the E.U., to provide two competing examples, are following very different pathways in this regard. The U.S. is currently (and we must stress currently, because the election of Democrat-led Administration *may* alter the course) operating on the basis of non-financial information as being a distraction from the true goal of a corporation or investor—profit maximisation. So much so, the Department for Labor recently outlawed institutional investors from even considering non-financial information. Furthermore, the SEC is unashamedly against enforcing standards for non-financial information disclosure, instead leaving it to the market to resolve. In the E.U., the bloc is hurtling towards a legislative turning point, as its *Green Deal* suite of legislative Acts begin to take shape. In fact, the E.U. is about to enforce the disclosure of non-financial information from mid-to-large sized public corporations. Similarly, the Regulation that forces 'financial market participants'—ranging from insurance, pension, and investment management firms, amongst others—to detail how they incorporate the concept of ESG into their practices, will also come into force during 2021.[22] Although there is no enforced standard, the development is in marked contrast to the U.S. Nevertheless, the push for a standard for non-financial information disclosure is continuing, albeit unsuccessfully.

Advocates of the need for standardisation have argued that the ability to compare non-financial information would elevate the development of the post-Crisis financial arena.[23] As the process is voluntary, there have been a small number of standard-setters who have attempted to fulfil the role of forging the path for the non-financial marketplace; those are the Global Reporting Initiative (GRI), the Sustainability Accounting Standards Board (SASB), the Task Force on Climate-Related Financial Disclosures (TCFD), and the Committee of Sponsoring Organisations of the Treadway Commission (COSO). What these organisations do, in different ways, is develop guidance on how data should be selected, what should/could be considered as 'material', criteria for assessments, processes for scenario testing, and a number of other aspects.[24] However, we can see the problem immediately; how can one obtain consistency and comparability when there are so many standards being touted by the market? Whilst the SASB, for one, has argued that each is a tool for investors to use at any given time and that there should not be just one standard,[25] the effect is still the same—the request and requirement of the market go unanswered. There are also a number of certification-based standards, like those from the Fair Labor Association, the International Organisation for Standardisation (ISO), and the Social Accountability International organisation, but yet again the same problem occurs. Whilst the GRI is widely accepted as a leading standard-setter, is not agreed-upon nor enforced by regulation.[26] Interestingly, in the U.S., Ho explains how the major formal driver for initiating the establishment of a standard—via shareholder proposals because regulators do not want to intervene—would be shut down by the companies' leadership because of the prohibition on shareholders 'micro-managing' corporate entities.[27]

On the other side of the equation, the CSSs are slaves to the information provided to them, and are well aware of this bind.[28] With the divergency present in the CSS universe anyway, as we saw in Chapter 2, not having standardised information upon which ratings and rankings can be developed, only serves to intensify that divergence. The result is that investors will always be exposed to divergent ESG ratings because of this systemic failure.[29] We know that investors are pleading for comparability, and it seems that there is nothing the CSSs can do to meet that need because the information they acquire, or receive, varies so widely and has different groundings across the board. This is a major hurdle that needs to be overcome. However, there is an underlying, more systemic requirement of the usage of third-parties that investors need, and it is potentially in understanding this systemic need that the potential victor from between the CSS and the credit rating industry comes into view.

5.3 Signalling

Credit rating agencies have been around for a lot longer than CSSs. We know this, having assessed each industry's history and trajectory. However, *why* the credit rating industry have endured for so long is not because of preference. It is merely because the agencies fulfil a fundamental role in the marketplace; entities need to signal to each other. Not only this, but it is often far more cost-effective to have a third-party signal a message, whether explicitly or implied. Let me give you an example: How would an issuer signal to the market that they are worthy of investment? They could tell the market via a press release, say, but why would anybody believe them? They could provide particular details about why they are worth investing in, but what if that revelation revealed commercially sensitive information? What if the investors were not set up to integrate and understand that information fully? The result would be a multitude of inefficiency. This is just one example out of many that form the underlying dynamic of the rating arena, and the relationships between associated parties.

What lays at the heart of the theory of Signalling (often spelled Signaling in American English) is the concept of 'information asymmetry'. This core concept must be understood if one is to understand the need for rating agencies, and why they endure and develop. Information Asymmetry, in simple terms, describes the dynamic whereby one party has access to more information than another party, for whatever reason. In our scenario, it is the investor who suffers from the dynamic of asymmetric information; the investor cannot know, for sure, the ins-and-outs of the issuer's business. Irrespective of what happens, the issuer knows their business better than anybody. To resolve that, investors rely on a number of methods to bridge that gap. These range from consulting publicly available information, and predominantly utilising third parties like rating entities and auditors. This is because third parties can get closer to the issuers than investors can, and they can simultaneously reduce any costs arising from duplication, i.e. the issuer need only liaise with a small number of third parties to release the necessary information, rather than for every investor.

Some have suggested that intermediaries are important in bridging that asymmetric gap,[30] but in reality they are much more than that; they are vital. Therefore, when we understand what 'Signalling Theory' argues, then we see that intermediaries have to be more than 'important'. Bird and Bird helpfully simplify the concept of Signalling Theory when they explain that:

> More broadly, signalling theory is concerned with how and why organisms exchange otherwise hidden information about each other or the world around them.[31]

At the core of the Theory lies a lineage, but for our purposes it needs to be interrogated. Connelly et al. describe the lineage as consisting of four distinct phases:

- Signaller (person, product, or firm that has an underlying quality and needs to convince others of it);
- The signal is sent to the Receiver;
- The Receiver observes and interprets the signal. The Receiver then chooses the person, product, or firm if it is satisfied with the signal;
- Feedback is sent to the Signaller regarding their signal.[32]

However, there are a number of issues with this suggested process. For example, what if the Receiver does not have the skill, or incentive to understand the signal? This is why I argue that, particularly in our arena that we are looking at, alterations need to be made. In our amended understanding:

- Signaller (person, product, or firm that has an underlying quality and needs to convince others of it);
- The information on the underlying quality is sent to a third-party;
- The third-party sends the signal to the Receiver;
- The Receiver observes and interprets the third-party's signal, and chooses to absorb the signal;
- Feedback is sent to the Signaller via investment (in whatever form).

Signalling Theory has a small number of founders, because the theory was being developed and played with by scholars such as George Akerlof, Michael Spence, and Joseph Stiglitz in the early 1970s.[33] All three won the Nobel Prize for their contributions to Economics, but Spence's early work is a fine example of the relatability of the Theory. He utilises the field of Human Resources to demonstrate the Theory and Connelly et al. explain his thesis for us:

> In his formulation of signaling theory, Spence utilized the labor market to model the signaling function of education. Potential employers lack information about the quality of job candidates. The candidates, therefore, obtain education to signal their quality and reduce information asymmetries. This is presumably a reliable signal because lower quality candidates would not be able to withstand the rigors of higher education. Spence's model stands in contrast to human capital theory because he deemphasizes the role of education for increasing worker productivity and focuses instead on education as a means to communicate otherwise unobservable characteristics of the job candidate.[34]

Another example could be when a firm confirms that it will be paying dividends; the act of doing so signals a strength of the firm that, before the publication of the plans, could not have been known by many. The opposite is true for when a firm may declare a profit warning.

Signalling theory is widely applied. It has been used to explain the relationships within anthropology, sociology, economics, law, and even the plumage of the peacock.[35] In relation to economic theory, it was a defining moment. Before the theoretical discovery, it was thought that informational balance in the marketplace could be perfect. Therefore, when the scholars developed this idea, it 'changed the paradigm of information economics and deeply affected the findings of the past'. The theory is based on four particular recognitions: 'it is now recognised that information is imperfect, obtaining information can be costly, there are important asymmetries of information, and the extent of information asymmetries is affected by actions of firms and individuals'.[36] Interestingly, Wolf adds to this understanding when she states that:

> In its essence, signalling theory is about information asymmetry, defined as one side knowing more than the other side… this information asymmetry causes uncertainty on the receiver side regarding quality, service, characteristics, qualifications, etc. and uncertainty is related to higher information costs and higher perceptions of risk. Signalling theory highlights two types of information, information about quality and information about intent. In the first case, one side has no complete information on the characteristics of the other side. In the second case, one side is not fully aware of the behaviour or the intentions of another party.[37]

This understanding positions the parties in the given interaction nicely, and they all have different requirements and incentives. The signaller is in possession of potentially valuable information, but is theoretically unable to communicate the impact of the knowledge directly; take Spence's example of the job applicant with a degree—would the employer believe the applicant if they simply said that they were capable of withstanding the pressures of the job? The receiver, for their part, needs to be willing and able to understand the signal, and then have the capacity to incorporate it or act on it. In Spence's example, what if they employer has never been to a University? How would they know the signal being sent via the obtaining of a degree? They may be able to assume, but that assumption can create inefficiency. In our arena, the receiver—the investor—may not understand the signal being sent directly from the issuer, or may not trust it. Also, as Baret and Helrich correctly identify, in our arena there is the problem of agency, whereby the actual holders of the resources—the end investor, or the pension holder—is not inclined to understand the information sent from the signaller because they are not in a position to act on it.[38] Therefore, reporting sustainability-related information is a start, but can it really be enough?

The answer is no. This is why Spence himself remarked in the early 2000s that 'generally, on the side of outsourcing is the likelihood that certain functions can be performed better by specialists who have the advantages of economies of focus and scale'.[39] There are a number of reasons however as to why our CSSs and credit rating agencies are not outsourced by choice, but by function. The first is that they provide translations of the underlying quality that the signaller is trying to communicate. These translations are easy to assimilate (particularly in the case of credit rating agencies), which then allow institutional investors and their management to communicate their investment processes and decisions with their underlying investor base, and also with regulators (many institutional investors are forced to only invest in highly rated securities because of their systemic importance). It is in the development of this translation that the economies of scale and focus come into play. The third parties also have the ability to work closely with the issuer and be privy to information that the investor could never be; in fact, the issuer-pays remuneration system actually encourages this. Then, that translation can, theoretically, be *trusted* because the third-party is independent. Trust is a key factor in the process of signalling.

The answer is no. This is why Spence himself remarked in the early 2000s that 'generally, on the side of outsourcing is the likelihood that certain functions can be performed better by specialists who have the advantages of economies of focus and scale'.[39] There are a number of reasons however as to why our CSSs and credit rating agencies are not outsourced by choice, but by function. The first is that they provide translations of the underlying quality that the signaller is trying to communicate. These translations are easy to assimilate (particularly in the case of credit rating agencies), which then allow institutional investors and their management to communicate their investment processes and decisions with their underlying investor base, and also with regulators (many institutional investors are forced to only invest in highly rated securities because of their systemic importance). It is in the development of this translation that the economies of scale and focus come into play. The third parties also have the ability to work closely with the issuer and be privy to information that the investor could never be; in fact, the issuer-pays remuneration system actually encourages this. Then, that translation can, theoretically, be *trusted* because the third-party is independent. Trust is a key factor in the process of signalling.

Third-party independence is an important facet in many walks of life. Baron provides a fantastic example with the rile of the media, in that 'News agencies' credibility is based on the belief that they are not personally involved in the story and offer an objective third-party perspective. When that third-party independence is compromised, the credibility of the story and the storyteller is quickly compromised as well.[40] In the financial sector, the *reliability* of information is a 'central pillar of an efficient capital market', and the delivery of that reliable information is vital, as long as the vehicles that deliver that information maintain a 'minimum level of independence'.[41] However, the example of the credit rating industry is somewhat of a 'theory-buster', because whatever theory is applied to it the industry finds a way to prove it wrong. For example, Leyens describes the process whereby:

> An intermediary will only be made use of by the acquirer, however, if the additional information can be expected to be credible. This credibility in turn depends on a minimum level of independence from the offeror. Accordingly, as a first element of independence, it can be said that the intermediary must not act in the interest of the offeror of the information.[42]

Mattarocci adds to this, arguing that the rating of a rating agency is only an 'opinion' (as it is legally designated) based on information available at the time, and investors can only ever be sure of the accuracy of the rating at some point in the future, long after their interest in the rating expires.[43] Therefore, we have an industry that is used because its outputs are supposed to be accurate, and because they are deemed independent from the issuers. Yet, the vast majority of assessments conclude that the informational value of ratings is weak, and the industry is far too close to the issuers via the issuer-pays model and have, in the past, actively colluded with issuers against the position of the investors (the cause for the post-Crisis financial settlements). Furthermore, during times of market bubbles, when the investors need the information from the agencies the most, it has been widely observed that issuers apply more pressure than usual to agencies to rate favourably, and that the agencies comply willingly.[44] Then, on top of all that, the rating agencies are almost unique in the lack of independence they can display without being regulated to the contrary, because as Sangiorgi and Spatt identify, unlike auditors the rating agencies are still permitted to offer incredibly lucrative ancillary services which are also particularly strong sources of conflicts of interests.[45] The authors also argue that the decision to settle with the rating agencies in the wake of the Crisis rather than break up the agencies, in a similar manner to what happened to the auditors after the Enron/WorldCom scandals, further demonstrates the diverging treatment.

This is all true. The agencies are not fully independent, but do have a strong enough veneer of independence. There are also mandated internal mechanisms designed to reduce the impact of inherent conflicts of interests. However, it does not matter much. The rating agencies and CSSs provide a function that overrides objections to their payment models. The ability to signal to other parties, particularly in a field beset by complexity, is of the utmost importance; nothing can come before it. Yet, the issue with ESG factors is that they are proving difficult to translate and communicate is such an easy manner. The underlying aspects are too fluid, too subjective, and have differing time horizons. If the investors *need* comparable information then, the CSSs and their dispersed and relatively new industry will simply add to the problem. This is not to say that their offerings are inherently weaker than what the credit rating agencies can provide, it is just that their industrial model is not optimal for the needs of the investors. The industrial model of the credit rating agencies on the other hand provides us with a clear example of why the credit rating agencies continue to prosper despite so many transgressions.

5.4 The Relevance of the Natural Oligopoly

The economic study of oligopolistic marketplaces is an extensive one. The word Oligopoly is derived from the Greek word 'oligos' and essentially translates to 'few sellers'.[46] The study has a number of defined contributors who have developed the concept, ranging from Augustin Cournot and Joseph Bertrand, to Heinrich Freiherr von Stackelberg.[47] The theoretical development has been concerned with the cause of competition between members of a marketplace, whether that may be based on price or quantity. Stackelberg moved the theory onwards when he considered the interplay between the members, i.e. how one firm acts in relation to another firm. In a duopoly, this is a particularly important consideration. He suggested that in a duopoly or oligopoly, firms will either follow a leader (known as the Stackelberg equilibrium), each firm will choose to be a follower (known as the Cournot equilibrium), or each firm will compete to be the leader (known as Stackelberg warfare). Therefore, some element of collusion is applied to the concept, although it has been argued that conscious collusion is more probable in a duopoly rather than an oligopoly.[48]

There are some excellent and arguably necessarily complicated definitions of what a 'natural oligopoly' is, which is different to a normal oligopoly.[49] Essentially, a natural oligopoly is 'a market in which the number of firms that minimises total industry cost is greater than one but not so large as to make the market competitive'.[50] Natural oligopolies have been identified as consisting of a small number of large players, with a fringe of niche players outside of the leadership of the oligopoly.[51] For a natural oligopoly to be present, there has to be distinctive barriers to entry; as Hall and Lieberman note, if one wants to identify an oligopoly, one need only search for barriers to entry.[52] Hall and Lieberman demonstrate that there are a number of barriers which may be present in an oligopoly:

- Economies of Scale—If the minimum efficient scale requires a firm to have a large share of the market, then smaller firms cannot compete. Examples could be airlines, textbook publishers, and passenger jet manufacturers.
- Reputation—As the scholars say, a new entrant may just be too new for the market. Reputation is usually built over time, so the oldest protagonists will receive favour over newer entrants. A new entrant may want to build that reputation, but it will likely require large advertising outlays and lower revenues for the initial period, which is often off putting as the leading levels of revenue are not guaranteed after all that investment.
- Strategic Barriers—Oligopolists could negotiate deals with suppliers or distributors, or maintain excess capacity to flood the market and scupper the new entrant's ability to derive revenues from the market. They could also utilise their larger resources to increase advertising spending to a level that dwarfs the new entrant's impact.
- Legal Barriers—There can be regulatory licences and grants that effectively ring fence an oligopoly; medicine is a good example of this approach.

One of the biggest differences between monopolies and oligopolies, and also something which presents difficulties for economic scholars, is the understanding that firms are *interdependent*. This means that they monitor each other and take the appropriate action to maintain the oligopoly. A good example of this is the credit rating oligopoly, where S&P and Moody's essentially lead a duopoly (though it is always referred to as an oligopoly with Fitch); The two leaders changing their remuneration models within a short time of each other in the late 1960s and early 1970s, and Fitch settling with CalPERS for damning documents against the Big Two signals a duopoly. One of the results of this organisational structure is that the leading firms can essentially exert pressure on the marketplace without a formal cartel agreement.[53] Whilst barriers to entry may differ, there is a succinct question that can help one locate any barriers: 'what factors enable an incumbent or incumbents to earn profits in excess of normal profit levels while other equally or more efficient firms are excluded'.[54]

If we consider the credit rating oligopoly, then something becomes immediately evident; none of the proposed reasons for barriers to entry directly apply to the industry. There have been regulations that have forced the ratings on the market, but that has been withdrawn and the usage of the ratings has increased. The economies of scale argument do not apply, and if reputation is a key facet then why has the usage of the Big Two increased since the Financial Crisis? The leading credit rating agencies have not formed any formal partnerships with issuers. So, why then is there an oligopolistic structure in the credit rating industry? The answer is simply the different elements of this chapter. As Schroeter says, 'the market for credit ratings is an investor-driven natural oligopoly'.[55]

One of the key elements of post-Crisis regulations was the legislative and regulatory aim of increasing competition. However, this has failed completely, and the reason is simple. Schroeter describes why perfectly:

> The evidence suggests that the decisive barrier to entry rather resides on the rating market's demand-side, namely the investors' preference for a market with only a few rating suppliers: Since a central reason for credit ratings' usefulness to investors is that they reduce complexity by distilling a wealth of market information into an easy-to-process rating symbol, this advantage would be lost again, had the investors to assimilate and process ratings from a large number of competing credit rating agencies. Financial markets frequented by investors with a limited capacity to assimilate

> and process information – the latter being a natural characteristic of real-world investors, although not reflected in the theoretical economic model of an efficient market – therefore always result in an investor-driven natural oligopoly of rating suppliers, making attempts to increase the number of relevant credit rating agencies futile.[56]

The OECD, in confirming all of the above, conclude that 'the market for fundamental credit ratings cannot sustain a large number of agencies and tends towards a natural oligopoly'.[57] Therefore, there is only really one outcome that we can reach: the market will dictate the trajectory of any rating market. It must be on the market's terms.

The implication of this outcome is stark for the CSS universe. We have seen that the market, at the moment, is not happy with the service they are offering. Their divergent, changing, and unstandardised offering simply does not fit with that the mainstream investor base *need*. There is no evidence to suggest that the investors will change their requirements to suit the nascent CSS universe, nor will they wait. For the credit rating agencies, they appear to have the structural elements to satisfy the market's requirements, but they do not necessarily have the specialised knowledge that the market needs. We are at the crossroads for ESG integration and one of these two industries will need to service the mainstream investor base, because each dipping their toe is inefficient. However, neither are completely ready. The question now that we have understood the investor base and the development of the ESG concept, the CSS universe and the credit rating industry is 'who will triumph' in the battle to serve the mainstream investors?

Notes

1. A perfect example of the exuberance and subsequent exploitation of the retail investor can be found in the story of Charles E. Mitchell, the president of National City Bank: see Edmund Wilson, 'Charles E. Mitchell' in Charles D. Ellis and James R. Vertin, *Wall Street People: True Stories of the Great Barons of Finance* (Wiley 2003).
2. For more on the trajectory of the American retail investor see Julia Ott, *When Wall Street Met Main Street: The Quest for an Investors' Democracy* (Harvard University Press 2011); for an interesting historical analysis of the 'New Deal' era and its effects, see Kiran K. Patel, *The New Deal: A Global History* (Princeton University Press 2017).

3. John C. Coffee, 'The Future of Disclosure: ESG, Common Ownership, and Systemic Risk' (2020) European Corporate Governance Institute: Law Working Paper No. 541/2020 https://scholarship.law.columbia.edu/cgi/viewcontent.cgi?article=3684&context=faculty_scholarship 2.
4. Ibid. 4.
5. Jill Solomon, *Corporate Governance and Accountability* (Wiley 2020) 237.
6. Ellen Quigley, 'Universal Ownership in the Anthropocene' (2019) SSRN https://papers.ssrn.com/sol3/papers.cfm?abstract_id=3457205#:~:text=Universal%20Ownership%20Theory%20describes%20large,3457205%20Page%202%20economy%20and 5.
7. (n 4).
8. Nick Robins, 'Sizing the Climate Economy' in Iveta Cherneva, *The Business Case for Sustainable Finance* (Routledge 2012) 100.
9. Austin Moss, James P. Naughton, and Clare Wong, 'The Irrelevance of ESG Disclosure to Retail Investors: Evidence from Robinhood' (2020) SSRN https://papers.ssrn.com/sol3/papers.cfm?abstract_id=3604847 20.
10. James P. Hawley and Andrew T. Williams, *The Rise of Fiduciary Capitalism: How Institutional Investors Can Make Corporate America More Democratic* (University of Pennsylvania Press 2000) 1.
11. Julie Segal, 'There's an Oligopoly in Asset Management. This Researcher Says It Should Be Broken Up' (2020) Institutional Investor (Nov 24). https://www.institutionalinvestor.com/article/b1pcwthdczlycw/There-s-an-Oligopoly-in-Asset-Management-This-Researcher-Says-It-Should-Be-Broken-Up.
12. Jakob de Haan, Sander Oosterloo, and Dirk Schoenmaker, *European Financial Markets and Institutions* (Cambridge University Press 2009) 181.
13. (n 3) 10.
14. (n 3) 7.
15. Robert A.G. Monks and Nell Minow, *Corporate Governance* (3rd ed, Blackwell Publishing 2004) 120.
16. Ibid. 144.
17. (n 6) 8.
18. Beate Sjåfjell, *Towards a Sustainable European Company Law: A Normative Analysis of the Objectives of EU Law, with the Takeover Directive as a Test Case* (Kluwer 2009) 76.
19. SASB 2016 Symposium, 'The Next Wave of ESG Integration: Lessons from Institutional Investors' (2017) 29 *Journal of Applied Corporate Finance* 2 10–109, 35.
20. Amir Amel-Zadeh and George Serafeim, 'Why and How Investors Use ESG Information: Evidence from a Global Survey' (2018) 74 *Financial Analysts Journal* 3 87–103, 93.

21. (n 3) 7.
22. Regulation (EU) 2019/2088 of the European Parliament and of the Council on Sustainability-Related Disclosures in the Financial Services Sector.
23. Alfonso Del Giudice and Silvia Rigamonti, 'Does Audit Improve the Quality of ESG Scores? Evidence from Corporate Misconduct' (2020) 12 *Sustainability* 5670, 5682.
24. Todd Cort and Daniel Esty, 'ESG Standards: Looming Challenges and Pathways Forward' (2020) 33 *Organization & Environment* 4 491–510, 503.
25. Tim Mohinof and Jean Rogers, 'SASB and GRI Pen Joint Op-Ed on Sustainability Reporting Synchronicity' (2017). https://www.sasb.org/blog/blog-sasb-gri-pen-joint-op-ed-sustainability-reporting-sychronicity/.
26. Susanne Arvidsson, 'An Expose of the Challenging Practice Development of Sustainability Reporting: From the First Wave to the EU Directive (2014/95/EU)' in Susanne Arvidsson, *Challenges in Managing Sustainable Business: Reporting, Taxation, Ethics and Governance* (Springer 2018) 12.
27. Virginia H. Ho, 'Non-financial Reporting & Corporate Governance: Explaining American Divergence & Its Implications for Disclosure Reform' (2020) *Accounting, Economics, and Law: A Convivium* 1251.
28. Michael S. Pagano, Graham Sinclair, and Tina Yang, 'Understanding ESG Ratings and ESG Indexes' in Sabri Boubaker, Douglas Cumming, and Duc K. Nguyen, *Research Handbook of Finance and Sustainability* (Edward Elgar 2018) 359.
29. Florian Berg, Julian F. Koelbel, and Roberto Rigobon, 'Aggregate Confusion: The Divergence of ESG Ratings' (2019) MIT Sloan School Working Paper 5822-19, 33.
30. Marguerite Mendell and Erica Barbosa, 'Impact Investing: A Preliminary Analysis of Emergent Primary and Secondary Exchange Platforms' (2012) 3 *Journal of Sustainable Finance & Investment* 2 111–123, 113.
31. Douglas W. Bird and Rebecca Bliege Bird, 'Signalling Theory and Durable Symbolic Expression' in Bruno David and Ian J. McNiven *The Oxford Handbook of the Archaeology and Anthropology of Rock Art* (OUP 2019) 347.
32. Brian L. Connelly, S. Trevis Certo, R. Duane Ireland, and Christopher R. Reutzel, 'Signaling Theory: A Review and Assessment' (2011) 37 *Journal of Management* 1 39–67, 44.
33. Sandra Wolf, *Signaling Family Firm Identity: Family Firm Identification and Its Effects on Job Seekers' Perceptions About a Potential Employer* (Springer 2017) 32.
34. (n 31) 42.

35. Patrick Bolton and Mathias Dewatripont, *Contract Theory* (MIT Press 2005) 126.
36. (n 32).
37. Ibid.
38. Pierre Baret and Vincent Helrich, 'The "Trilemma" of Non-financial Reporting and Its Pitfalls' (2018) 23 *Journal of Management and Governance* 485–511.
39. Michael Spence, 'Signaling in Retrospect and the Informational Structure of Markets' (2002) 92 *The American Economic Review* 3 434–459, 455.
40. Gerald R. Baron, *Now Is Too Late: Survival in an Era of Instant News* (FT Press 2003) 307.
41. Patrick C. Leyens, 'Intermediary Independence: Auditors, Financial Analysts and Rating Agencies' (2011) 11 *Journal of Corporate Law Studies* 1 33–66, 33.
42. Ibid. 36.
43. Gianluca Mattarocci, *The Independence of Credit Rating Agencies: How Business Models and Regulators Interact* (Academic Press 2013) xvii.
44. (n 40) 45.
45. Francesco Sangiorgi and Chester Spatt, *The Economics of Credit Rating Agencies* (Now Publishers 2018) 75. For more on the impact of ancillary services on the provision of rating services, see Daniel Cash, *Regulation and the Credit Rating Agencies: Restraining Ancillary Services* (Routledge 2018).
46. William A. McEachern, *Economics: A Contemporary Introduction* (Cengage Learning 2011) 226.
47. For more on this development, see Daniel Cash, 'Can Regulatory Intervention Save the Sustainability Rating Industry?' (2021) 42 *Business Law Review* 1.
48. Steffan Huck, Hans-Theo Normann, and Jorg Oechssler, 'Two Are Few and Four Are Many: Number Effects in Experimental Oligopolies' (2004) 53 *Journal of Economic Behaviour & Organization* 435–46, 444.
49. Avner Shaked and John Sutton, 'Natural Oligopolies' (1983) 51 *Econometrica* 5 1469–1483.
50. William W. Sharkey, *The Theory of Natural Monopoly* (Cambridge University Press 1982) 145.
51. Thomas Gehrig, 'Natural Oligopoly and Customer Networks in Intermediated Markets' (1996) 12 *International Journal of Industrial Organisation* 101–118, 101.
52. Robert E. Hall and Marc Lieberman, *Economics: Principles and Applications* (Cengage 2007) 302.
53. Sigrid Stroux, *US and EC Oligopoly Control* (Kluwer 2004) 8.
54. Ibid. 23.

55. Ulrich G. Schroeter, 'Credit Ratings and Credit Rating Agencies' in Gerard Caprio, *Handbook of Key Global Financial Markets, Institutions, and Infrastructure* (Academic Press 2013) 387.
56. Ibid.
57. OECD, *Bank Competition and Financial Stability* (OECD Publishing 2011) 25.

CHAPTER 6

Who Will Triumph?

The question of which industry will triumph in the battle to serve the mainstream investor base in one that needs a lot of contextualisation. Whether they are even in conflict could be questioned. However, this book aims to suggest that they *may*, and I would go even further to say that is *highly likely* that they will at some point. The main reason for that assumption is that the investor base, as we saw in the last chapter, *needs* certain things and they will ensure that they get what they need. Then, the question of 'who will succeed' becomes more plausible because the investor base simply does not want a dispersed service sector, offering dispersed sources of information. They need a streamlined, organised, and efficient industrial model to meet their requirements.

There is one issue that stands out more than most in the sector, and that is *disclosure*. The information that the investors want is housed within the companies that they are investing in, and before the question gets to how that information may be interpreted, categorised, and *standardised*, the first step is to obtain the necessary information. In that regard, the development is of crucial importance to the investor base and, I argue, of even more importance to the potential trajectory of the CSSs and the credit rating agencies looking to serve the investor base. In this chapter, we shall examine those developments in much greater detail.

In the last Chapter we learned more about the underlying dynamics of the investor base and what they *need*. I strongly argue that the sole reason

D. Cash, *Sustainability Rating Agencies vs Credit Rating Agencies*, Palgrave Studies in Impact Finance,
https://doi.org/10.1007/978-3-030-71693-6_6

for regulatory failures in the past is because of a misunderstanding of this underlying dynamic. It could be the case that legislators need to preserve authority by acting, largely irrespective of the chances of success. I say this because attempting to promote competition in the rating sector is misguided at best and imprudent at worst. We know why this is because of what we learned in the last Chapter. However, what if this were to happen again? What effect may that have on the trajectory of the two rating arenas?

To find out who may triumph in the battle to serve the mainstream investor base, we need to assess what may be the most impactful external developments. For us, that is the development of non-financial informational disclosure regimes, or the lack thereof. In the U.S. and the E.U., we have two perfect conflicting approaches, although the context for both approaches makes perfect sense for those particular entities. For the CSS universe, developments in this field are perhaps their only lifeline; improving the quality and reliability of information that the CSSs can then utilise could be the spark that brings the market closer towards the CSSs. It could potentially elevate the market to the levels of the credit rating agencies. However, it is a double-edged sword because if that informational flow is improved and the CSSs still cannot deliver what the investor base needs from them, it could be a death knell. On the opposing side, the credit rating agencies could stand to profit massively if they can channel any improvement in the informational flow through their oligopolistic model, which rightly or wrongly suits the investor base perfectly; would it really take too much change for the credit rating agencies to perform the services the CSSs perform *and* provide ratings?

To learn more about these developments and their impact, we need to start at a global level, and then descend down to the two regulatory powerhouses who are shaping the path forwards for associated industries.

6.1 Standard Setting at the Global Level

The problem of needing to set standards for what may count as impactful in the financial meaning of sustainability is a widely identified one. Issues such as what business practices may impact on the sustainability of a company, what 'materiality' means, and how such issues should be communicated are a global issue. Therefore, initiatives have been developed to meet this need and set overarching standards that businesses and associated industries can follow. The obvious problem is that because it is widely identified, a number of initiatives have been developed. When one of the fundamental elements that is needed to push the concept of sustainability forwards is comparability and convergence, this is not entirely helpful. Nevertheless, this has not stopped the development of a number of standard-setters.

In the overarching realm, there are two particular standard-setters worth mentioning: the Global Reporting Initiative (GRI) and the Sustainability Accounting Standards Board (SASB). These two standard-setters offer different things, although market participants have been found not to be overly sure what the difference is. The GRI was formed in 1997 by the Coalition for Environmentally Responsible Economies (CERES) together with the United Nations Environment Programme (UNEP) and the SASB was formed in 2012 by a number of private individuals, with one particularly central founder being Michael Bloomberg.

Rupley et al. note that the concept of voluntarily reporting on sustainability issues can be traced back to the Exxon Valdez Oil Spill in 1989[1]—when one of Exxon's oil tankers ran aground in Alaska and spilled more than 10 million gallons of Oil—because, in response, a number of social investment professionals came together to form CERES. Their first act was to develop and disseminate 10 'principles' that ranged from environmentally-friendly business practices, and also specific disclosure regimes. In 1997, when the GRI was launched by CERES, the initiative had the objective of being:

> [L]ike the Financial Accounting Standards Board in the U.S. and standard-setting bodies elsewhere in the financial world with a single but vital mission – to generate consensus among global constituencies regarding which corporate sustainability attributes should be measured and how they should be reported.[2]

One of the key aims of the initiative was to allow not only for cross-company but also cross-industry comparisons.[3] Therefore, transparency is a central aim.[4] It aimed to become one of the leaders in providing for guidelines and principles to be followed,[5] and is widely understood to be the standard-setter for the sector. Whilst its dominance is widely accepted, there are criticisms that are levelled at the GRI, with the most apt one perhaps being the suggestion that the GRI has 'arrived at its maturation stage facing a plethora of challenges, many of which are grounded in the strategies adopted by its founder'.[6]

The GRI has a number of standards, and for a variety of sectors and issues (like Waste, Tax, Occupational Health and Safety, and Water Usage). However, although criticism may be a natural accompaniment to being recognised as a leader, there are some particularly important suggestions that have been made regarding shortcomings with the GRI and the usage of its service. One is that voluntarily adhering to the standards can have a positive effect on the company in question, so there is an incentive to do so. Whilst that is positive, it has been argued that we should be suspicious of companies who may use the GRI to gain marketing benefits through greenwashing.[7] A related criticism is that the GRI only focuses on an informational perspective, rather than an impact-based perspective; Revelli says, in relation to this argument, that 'a company should be judged on what it actually does rather than what it says it is doing'.[8] The assurance of the information voluntarily provided is of real concern, as we shall see shortly.

Perhaps an abstract criticism, but certainly a valid one, is that the GRI do not utilise their position to push for a convergence on the meaning of terms like 'sustainability' or 'materiality'.[9] This is vitally important for the development of the field, because a lack of definition allows for divergence, but also with the GRI and SASB having different understandings of 'materiality', for example, that divergence is increased even more by entities that are supposed to be helping the development of the field.

The SASB was founded in 2011 by Jean Rogers and had a mission to 'establish and maintain industry-specific sustainability disclosure standards for listed companies in the United States'.[10] The initiative has had a number of high-profile Directors, ranging from Michael Bloomberg, Robert G. Eccles, and former SEC Chair Mary Schapiro. Grewal et al. note that the SASB has a perhaps more focused mission in that they exist to 'help businesses identify, manage and disclose the sustainability topics that matter most to their investors'.[11] Perhaps it is very similar, but the SASB certainly seems to aim to be more practical and targeted than the GRI. For example, in 2018 the SASB published a complete set of 77 industry standards that provide a complete set of globally applicable standards, all of which are concerned with identifying a minimal set of financial material sustainability topics.[12] This so-called Sustainable Industry Classification System comprises of 11 sectors that then divide into 77 industry standards. Overall, there are five broad sustainability categories that the SASB focus on: environment, social capital, human capital, business model and innovation, and leadership and governance.

They then apply a system of rankings, for want of a better terminology, than identifies each issue as having differing levels of impact.[13]

Though the GRI and the SASB are different and have different aims, they are often categories together just like I have done here. It has been suggested that the two are not in competition, but rather complement each other and are different tools for the market. Busco et al. argue that one of the biggest differences between them is the targeted audience. The GRI focus very much on stakeholders widely, whilst the SASB are predominantly focused on the financial impact, which is in the interests of the shareholders mainly (although I am sure one could argue that stakeholders benefit from an enriched company).[14] This focus on materiality is one that is widely identified, and as Eccles et al. further confirm:

> The different conceptualisations of materiality applied to ESG data that are most prominently referenced by companies and investors today are those of the GRI (Global Reporting Initiative) and the SASB (Sustainability Accounting Standards Board), respectively. Whereas SASB identifies material ESG issues for value-driven investment at the industry level based on their relevance to each firm's financial performance, GRI defines materiality as an externality, viewing as material that which reflects the organisation's most significant economic, environmental, and social impacts.[15]

It is therefore not surprising that yet another initiative has been developed, but this time to aid with the alignment in understandings. The Corporate Reporting Dialogue initiative recently launched the 'better alignment project', which aims to foster consistency between the variety of different frameworks that are available.

Yet, there are underlying problems which the initiatives have not resolved. Also, the multiplicity of initiatives that are designed to help the market is actively hurting it because multiplicity is the very last thing the market needs, and they have made this clear. One of the issues is that these initiatives, once formed, do not fold and the mass just keeps increasing. So, at an overarching and private level, there is multiplicity. But, there is an appetite for providing the framework(s) that the market wants. However, on the geopolitical level, there are wildly varying approaches affecting the marketplace.

6.2 The U.S. Experience

The United States, standing as the world's leading economy, has the potential to set the tone when it comes to financial movements. In the U.S., there exists a culture that favours free enterprise, limited regulatory intervention, and ultimately the focus is on profit and 'financial materiality'. This is witnessed throughout the history of the country, but with regard to the issue of non-financial informational disclosure, the cultural influence is acute. Nevertheless, there is evidence to suggest that there is a growing appetite for the integration of ESG into investment practices. In 2018, investors representing more than $5 trillion in Assets under Management (AuM) collaborated with corporate law scholars and to urge the SEC to undertake new rulemaking on ESG disclosure, and subsequently a climate risk disclosure bill was put forward before the Senate. In 2019, there were new proposals put forward by the House of Representatives regarding ESG disclosure.[16] This was a sea-change from just a few years earlier, as in 2016 the SEC asked for comments from the market as to whether they should be intervening more in the field on non-financial informational disclosure, and the market emphatically responded that they should not.[17]

There are a number of reasons for this. The first is that the SEC, whilst mandated to protect consumers and investors, does not want to become any more of a political player than it has to be; any overreach would be perceived to be the increasing politicisation of the SEC by businesses, which some have suggested would be particularly problematic given the U.S. framework.[18] The second reason is that the idea of non-financial information disclosure is incredibly contentious in the U.S., with one of the predominant fears being that of over-disclosure.[19] Over-disclosure means the fear that investors will be bombarded with too much information so as to defeat the point of non-financial disclosure, and also issuers will be forced to increase their level of disclosure which brings with it increased administration and compliance costs. The Supreme Court, in the *TSC Industries v Northway* and *Basic v Levinson* cases crystallised this idea and it has held ever since. Another reason is that, since 2016, the Trump Administration has embarked upon an extensive deregulation campaign, against which calls for more regulation regarding disclosure was always going to be met with short thrift—we wait to see whether the change in administration brings with it a change in emphasis regarding disclosure regulation.[20] Perhaps one of the most poignant reasons is the fear of liability. Ho explains that:

> For companies and some SEC commissioners, the prospect of new ESG disclosure mandates also raises many of the same concerns that specialized disclosures did about the potential costs of any expansion of reporting obligations, and the potential for firms to face increased exposure to disclosure-related litigation. Some of these concerns are heightened because of the nature of ESG information, for example: (i) The term "ESG" is subject to a wide range of interpretations, so its scope is potentially open-ended in the absence of narrowing definitions established by regulation or legislation. (ii) ESG information is often related to the business and legal risks associated with corporate operations and therefore will often be forward-looking and difficult to quantify or predict with certainty. (iii) Like cybersecurity risk, ESG risks are often described as "emerging," and therefore the materiality of particular ESG information may be more likely to change over time and to vary across issuers. (iv) Evidence from market participants suggests that which ESG issues are material to companies and their investors varies by industry sector. These features also raise challenges for regulators considering whether and how to craft appropriate disclosure rules.[21]

There is also the question of enforcing more disclosure is even necessary in the U.S. Ho presents the question on the basis that over 85% of companies on the S&P500 already produce voluntary sustainability reports. There are perhaps two responses to that suggestion: the first is that the enforced disclosure regime could potentially help with comparability, and not just the production rates because the regime could mandate which frameworks the sustainability reports had to attach themselves to, and reporting trends in the U.S. have been identified as focusing mostly on the 'E' and not necessarily the 'S',[22] which in the U.S. is an important factor with elements such as police brutality, amongst others, having a tangible effect upon business.

It is perhaps not accurate to paint the U.S. as without regulation, and the E.U.—as we shall see in the next section—as being of a more sophisticated regulatory mindset. The U.S. regulatory framework is well applied, and the SEC mandates disclosure on a number of levels. It is merely a case of very different foundations impacting the regulatory mentality and developments of the two entities. Also, there are different components to each entity with the U.S. having a much larger and impactful institutional investor cohort. For this reason, and whilst there are elements of SEC regulation in different sectors, the overriding mentality is that shareholder activism is the best way to 'move the markets', so to speak. For example, the recent interventions and voting strategies of the largest shareholders have been identified as the process working as it should, with Ho utilising the example of shareholder proposals presented to ExxonMobil in 2019 that were focused on having the company release more information.[23] The U.S. Chamber Foundation also speaks very highly of the work undertaken by leading institutional investors like BlackRock and State Street, with it also being highlighted that institutional investors (Vanguard is cited) are active in supporting organisations like the GRI and the SASB to help with the much needed standardisation of disclosure.[24]

This whole approach has been labelled as 'private ordering', and there have been a number of advantages cited for this approach and its supremacy. Private ordering means that private bodies, in this instance investors, issuers, and private standard-setting organisations, take the lead in organising the market. However, it is also a new word for self-regulation, in effect. Nevertheless, at least one advantage that makes absolute sense is that it is the private entities that know best what 'materiality' means to them. In being able to utilise this experience-driven knowledge, the private frameworks can, in theory, be more effective. Also, private standard-setting is much more flexible than a regulatory-driven framework could ever be, mostly because of the lower levels of bureaucracy. Allowing for a private standard-setting organisation to take charge of the development of non-financial disclosure allows for lower compliance costs for regulated entities, and much lower supervisory costs for the regulators themselves. It also, in the eyes of American participants, champions the notion of the free market and any perceived regulatory burden, which the SEC Chairman has intimated could translate into more listings in the U.S. capital markets.[25]

However, it is not all plain sailing. It has been found that the information contained in the voluntarily submitted annual reports are less than adequate on average. When it comes to the risk factors highlighted by companies, it has been argued that the reports 'often are generic and do not provide clear, concise, and insightful information'. Ho says that this is because of liability concerns, in that 'firms tend to limit the amount of forward-looking information they include in their annual reports, even though forward-looking information is most relevant to assessments of risk'. This may be so, but the SASB found in 2016 that 20% of all filings contained *no* ESG information whatsoever, and a further 40% only contained boilerplate language.[26] This is likely reduced in the time since, but not by very much.

Irrespective of the advantages or failings of the private ordering approach, the U.S. corporate law landscape has the approach entrenched within its fibre. Of particular importance is the central concept of 'materiality', and the American corporate landscape has perhaps been defined by the *TSC Industries* and then later by the *Basic* cases.[27] In *TSC*, the principle formed by the Court was that a piece of information becomes material 'if there is a substantial likelihood that a reasonable shareholder would consider it important in deciding how to vote'. The aim here was to develop a standard that reduced over-informing the shareholders for fear of reducing their ability to make sound decisions, but also for reducing any excess liability that companies may have faced in deciding what to disclose. Later, in *Basic*, the court extended this approach to the buying, selling, or holding of a security, i.e. the larger investor arena. The extension confirmed further the materiality test presented by Judge Marshall and the Court in *TSC*, so that the materiality principle filtered out 'essentially useless information that a reasonable investor would not consider significant, even as part of a larger "mix" of factors to consider'.[28] This is not to say that ESG-related issues are never to be considered, because in parts of numerous SEC regulations—like Regulation S-K—a company must disclose information regarding the protection of the environment on a company's expenditures, earnings, and competitive positioning, for example. But, clearly the general sustainability push happening at the moment does not fare well against this legal need to consider what are tangibly material aspects.

The SEC have decided not to enforce better disclosure standards in areas concerning ESG before because of the materiality standards set by the two cases.[29] Significant reports over the decades have supported the SEC in this refusal to encourage considering anything other than the financial materiality, like the 'Sommer Report'—a 1977 report by the Advisory Committee on Corporate Disclosure—that put forward the sentiment that 'the need to protect unsophisticated investors outweighed the disclosure objective of supplying the investment community with meaningful information'.[30] This immediately brings forward the question of whether this sentiment still holds, given that the institutional investor has now come to dominate the market, with 'unsophisticated investors' now simply aligning themselves with the much more resourced and experienced institutional investors, or indexes.

Leading SEC figures have confirmed over the years that 'in assessing materiality, the SEC staff takes the view that the reasonable investors generally focuses on matters that have affected, or will affect, a company's profitability and financial outlook'.[31] This concept of the 'reasonable investor' is one that has plagued corporate law and economics for a long time. In 2017, the U.S. Chamber of Commerce reported that 'an investor that bases its voting and investment decisions on promoting social or political goals is not a "reasonable" investor when it comes to what materiality means under the federal securities laws'.[32] What this does however is suggest that ESG integration is predominantly a social or political exercise, which is arguably not the case at all—investors have been clear that they generally consider the integration of ESG information into the investment decision-making process a positive thing, particularly for economic returns. Ho suggests that this is because the SEC have, for years, directed shareholders to frame any proposals regarding corporate operations and their impacts on the world as 'social' or 'policy' issues and now that sentiment has stuck, even though there is a plethora of evidence to suggest otherwise.

In terms of the dynamics of investing in the modern arena, the rise of the institutional investor has made laws relating to the fiduciary responsibilities of managers more important than ever. In the U.S., the law imposes upon the majority of States the concept of the 'sole interest rule', which means that the fiduciary must only act in the interest of the beneficiaries they are tasked with leading/protecting/serving.[33] Clearly, the easiest pathway for fiduciaries is to maintain a focus on the financial impact on the beneficiaries, which would limit their own exposure to liability under the said laws. However, Coffee has argued that it would be very unlikely for a court in the U.S. to hold a trustee liable for engaging with ESG integration when the obvious retort would be that doing so had the potential of being economically advantageous for the beneficiaries; Coffee follows this up with the observation that courts have been extremely hesitant to impose liability within the private markets (a theme across the Atlantic also), and that professional trustees are not viewed with the same suspicion as many of the other sectors in the financial arena.

There is criticism at every turn for the trajectory of the U.S. corporate arena—Ho argues that the risk of informational overload is 'largely irrelevant' and that articulated worries from companies are a 'false front' for the predictable concerns about regulatory burdens[34]—but the trajectory is continuing at a rapid pace. The most extreme example of this was witnessed in 2020, when the Department of Labor remarkably finalised a rule clarifying that 'pension fund managers must put retirees' financial interests first when allocating investments, rather than other concerns such as climate change or racial justice'. This incredible turn of events came just before the Trump Administration was voted out of office after a single term, and represented the nadir of the Administration's governance that was built upon such sentiments. As the CEO of the CFA Institute Marg Frankin said in the wake of the ruling, 'the Department's agenda to block consideration of anything ESG-related in the investment management process is a political gag-order'.[35] What this means is that the Department of Labor have directly tried to block one of the fundamental players in the American corporate arena from partaking in the sustainable finance movement; as the Country seemingly follows the free-market principle and trusts its market operators to push the economy forward, this approach of preventing market actors from investing in a certain way looks like one of the biggest political elements at play at the moment.

In reviewing the U.S. and its views towards ESG integration, we can see a highly institutionalised private market that is being entrusted with moving the market forward in a way that suits them. However, this is not exactly true, because the U.S. Government has been active in controlling the underlying sentiment, which reflects the Country's culture (arguably). The decision ofthe Department of Labor to *restrict* what an investor can do is a new development which likely will not hold given the incoming Administration, but perhaps the scene has been set for the United States to do things her way. Without passing judgement, it is just one way to approach this issue of developing a more sustainable financial marketplace. Across the Atlantic Ocean, the European Union is taking a very different approach. An interesting article in the Financial Times in October, entitled 'Investors should watch the transatlantic split on ESG closely',[36] examined the potential impact of the Biden Administration on the development of ESG integration in parallel to the large-scale aims of the E.U., and that is something we must do ourselves. The promise of the Biden Administration has not yet been seen, but the plans in Europe are already well under way.

6.3 The European Experience

Just as the U.S. has particular characteristics that stem from its collective culture, the same is true for the E.U. Its multi-Sovereign State make up makes for a particularly unique character, and impacts upon every element of the E.U.'s progression. There are a couple of relevant examples of this impact. One could be that it is difficult to present a conjoined approach to move forward with respect to, say, what institutional investors want in the bloc because not every country has a high rate of institutional investors within their national marketplace. If a policy objective was to focus on increasing the position of the institutional investor at any potential cost to the retail investor, then a number of southern and eastern countries within the bloc may not be too supportive. We shall look at this is more detail shortly.

However, there is a political dynamic constantly at play within the bloc that impacts almost every decision taken at the higher levels. The bloc is an entity in its own right, but consists of many different actors who have their own ambitions, understandings, cultures, and approaches. A clear example of this was the threat that the U.K's exit from the bloc would potentially have upon the unity of the other members, although this did not exactly play out as many right-wing actors had hoped. The E.U. has been trying to quell the potential contagion that could have arisen from 'brexit', but has faced issues recently in terms of applying their founding principles—like that of the 'rule of law'—to countries which are inching towards authoritarian rule, like Hungary and Poland.[37] This focus on the protection of the bloc from internal and external threats is understandable of course, but the extent of the legislative agenda over the past decade or so is in direct response to the threat of the Financial Crisis.[38] The Crisis affected the bloc's citizens like everywhere else, but the Sovereign Debt Crisis that followed was one of the largest threats the bloc had ever faced, and cost it an awful lot of money. Since then, the bloc has been hellbent on reducing the impact of a transgressive financial sector, with legislative approaches being witnessed in the fields of shareholder rights, banking, credit rating agencies, and many more. Yet, it is going further still. The bloc sees building a sustainable financial sector as crucial to its future and has thus developed a European *Green Deal*, which consists of a number of strands all designed to make the bloc carbon-neutral by 2050 and become a beacon for sustainable business. At the heart of that push is the move to focus on corporate disclosure.

The European Commission has stated that non-financial disclosure is a 'leverage for encouraging sustainable economic growth as well as improving "citizen and consumer trust and confidence in the Single Market"',[39] whilst also declaring its development as 'vital' to the aims of the bloc.[40] There are two pieces of regulatory action that are of interest. The first is the Regulation that focuses on the sustainability-related disclosures of financial market participants.[41] This Regulation is of real importance for our analysis, because it is forcing financial market participants like insurance entities, institutional investors, and investment managers to not only consider how they integrate the concept of sustainability and ESG into their practices, but also crucially how they transmit this to the investing public. However, the Regulation allows for flexibility for the participants in terms of what they consider to be *material*, and also to what standard they attach themselves. One of the easiest ways for the participants to publish information that can be understood will be to utilise the ratings of the CSSs and, potentially, the CRAs if their information is clear enough on the sustainability-related underpinnings (which, currently, they are not). This takes us back to the concept of 'signalling' that we were introduced to in the last Chapter.

The Regulation forms part of a larger regulatory movement by the E.U., as Busch explains:

> On 8 March 2018 the European Commission launched its Action Plan on Sustainable Finance ('Action Plan'). The Action Plan aims to: (i) reorient capital flows towards sustainable investment in order to achieve sustainable and inclusive growth; (ii) manage financial risks stemming from climate change, resource depletion, environmental degradation and social issues; and (iii) foster transparency and long-termism in financial and economic activity. In the Action Plan these aims are translated into ten concrete actions, including (1) strengthening sustainability-related disclosures and (2) clarifying sustainability-related fiduciary duties. Of course, the EU financial services sector has been the subject of detailed harmonised regulatory disclosure rules and harmonised regulatory fiduciary duties for many years, but until very recently harmonised regulatory sustainability-related (i) disclosure rules and (ii) fiduciary duties were lacking or in any event underdeveloped.
>
> The recently adopted Regulation on sustainability-related disclosures in the financial services sector (the 'Sustainable Finance Disclosure Regulation') aims to fill this gap by subjecting several players in the EU financial services sector to a harmonised set of regulatory sustainability-related (i)

> disclosure rules and (ii) fiduciary duties. The bulk of these new rules will apply from 10 March 2021.[42]

Both financial market participants and advisors must publish on their websites information related to how they integrate the understanding of 'sustainability risks' into their processes. Market participants must publish at least (i) information on the policies concerned with the identification of adverse sustainability impacts, (ii) a description of adverse sustainability impacts and the plans to counter them, (iii) brief summaries of engagement policies with other actors, and (iv) a reference to which codes and standards they align themselves to, as well as the degree of alignment to the Paris Agreement. Where they do not do any of this, they must explain why not, in line with the commonly-applied 'comply-or-explain' principle.

The next piece of Regulatory action is the Directive 2014/95/EU of the European Parliament, which is concerned with 'disclosure of non-financial and diversity information by certain large undertakings and groups'.[43] The Directive aims to enforce the publication, via a non-financial statement, from corporate entities with more than 500 employees information 'to the extent necessary for an understanding of the undertaking's development, performance, position and impact of its activity, relating to, as a minimum, environmental, social and employee matters, respect for human rights, anti-corruption and bribery matters'.

Before we assess the Directive itself, a comment from Tsagas and Villiers demonstrates the hope that is accompanying this legislative action, although they do provide for plenty of realistic critique in their work also:

> The Directive, with the required reforms, might go a step further and provide an alignment between the type of information disclosed and the audience it targets. It might also provide a common definition of concepts such as "materiality" and identify for whom the information is in fact "material", relying on economic, social and governance factors and Sustainable Development Goals for guidance.[44]

This is quite an aim. To align the information being disclosed with the needs of the market who need that information is a massive undertaking in itself, but to also set standards for elements which are proving almost impossible to standardise owing to the incredible divergence impacting upon such issues, is a gargantuan task.

Because of the interrelationship between the Regulation and the Directive, it is easy to become confused. The Regulation affects a certain number of industries indicated by the Regulation's preamble. The Regulation affects the whole of the E.U., and every industry affected with the Member States is bound by the Regulation's rules. The Directive, on the other hand, affects *all* companies with more than 500 employees. Because it is a Directive, this allows each Member State to interpret the rules of the Directive to fit their circumstance.

There are, of course, a number of different elements to the Directive, but those above offer a simplistic understanding. Essentially, the Directive aims to force large companies in the bloc to reveal what they consider to be impactful in terms of sustainability risks, how they integrate that understanding, and then what code or standard(s) they utilise to make those decisions. All sounds straightforward, but whilst there has been praise and hope for the bloc's agenda, there has been plenty of criticism and problems identified.

The first element to consider is that the E.U. chose to pursue this agenda via a *Directive*, rather than a regulation, decision, recommendation, or an opinion (the other forms of 'secondary law' within the European legal arsenal).[45] Aureli et al. explain that this was a purposeful and conscious move because of the effect it would have on those affected by the action, as well as the options that would be made available to the Member States:

> In achieving the aim of harmonisation, the EU chose to use a directive as a legal instrument, which leaves Member States to enjoy some freedom of choice, i.e. discretion, in the transposition. A regulation would have been binding in its entirety, while directives are binding with regard to the result to be achieved but leave the national actors with choice about form and methods. The use of a directive has allowed to avoid a one-size-fits-all approach and promoted a light-touch intervention in absence of a strong regulatory history on the matter.[46]

Jackson et al. confirm that target firms get almost complete discretion about their usual business practices, in that the Directive does not prescribe any one standard that must be adhered to in relation to non-financial disclosure.[47] The E.U. has provided the market with some potential avenues regarding what *may* be utilised, including: national frameworks; Union-based frameworks; and international frameworks like the UN Global Compact; the Guiding Principles on Business and Human Rights implementing the UN 'Protect, Respect and Remedy' framework; the OECD Guidelines for Multinational Enterprises; the International Organisation for Standardisation's ISO 26,000; the International Labour Organisation's Tripartite Declaration of principles; the Global Reporting Initiative (GRI), and others.[48]

Tsagas and Villiers discuss how the flexibility demonstrated above could be a positive and smart move by the E.U. It allows for companies to reveal *relevant* information, rather than having to tick a box and contribute 'noise' to the marketplace.[49] It also allows for an element of 'buy-in' from the market, as it allows them to be proactive and demonstrate their practice, rather than having it dictated to them. It also allows for the E.U. to move their agenda forward and hope then to develop some positive inertia for their wider objectives; perhaps any action in this field is better than no action. However, I am running out of examples of positives, because there are glaring issues which are so difficult to ignore.

In starting with the obvious issue, allowing for discretion in this field provides the clearest example of the problem facing everybody; how does one dictate to the market which standard to use when the underlying data and its usage is so variable and particular? The E.U. has chosen not to, and this has drawn criticism. As Tsagas and Villiers note, citing Ahern:

> However, there is also a downside to this approach. As Ahern remarks, "a regulatory approach which bows so far to market freedom invites a fragmented reporting landscape. The non-prescriptive approach to the reporting framework negates the possibility of a uniform approach being taken to sustainability reporting by companies within the EU. As a knock-on consequence, the ability to engage in meaningful cross company comparisons by stakeholders is likely to be significantly hampered." The "comply or explain" framework for the Directive exacerbates this problem. Again, in Ahern's words: "'Comply or explain' regimes are notorious for the variable quality of disclosures they evoke leading to an associated compliance deficit." Ahern concludes that "the perennial problem of poor disclosures is unlikely to be completely eradicated from a soft law regulatory regime."[50]

Aureli et al. agree, saying that 'discretion could lead to less comparability'. They also utilised the literature in explaining that in company disclosures, key aspects relating to risk management, human rights and corruption issues, and other aspects were missing from companies' reports. Others have argued that applying 'soft-law' to the practice of disclosure often just results in a symbolic management practice with very little useful output. There is also the problem of allowing Member States to implement the Directive as they see fit, with multiple instances of divergence being traditionally witnessed across the bloc in relation to disclosure.[51]

There has also been criticism of the process leading to the Directive, with it being suggested that the countries and organisations who were involved essentially weakened the process that resulted in the soft-law Directive. Also, it has been demonstrated that formal harmonisation does not necessarily translate into practical harmonisation, whilst the quality of what will be produced has been questioned. Jackson et al. find that whilst mandatory non-financial disclosure has had the effect in other instances of increasing the activity of firms, there is no evidence at all that mandatory non-financial disclosure leads to a corresponding decrease in irresponsible actions.[52] De Luca argues that, actually, reporting in this approach allows for a mask of sustainability to be presented to the marketplace, and that ultimately standardisation has simply not been achieved by this Directive.[53]

It is also the case that the target for the Directive is not adequate. Aiming for firms that have 500 employees or more equates to around 6000 entities in the E.U., but that is only a small proportion of the European marketplace. Owing to the diversity across the bloc, large swathes of the European business community will be missed by this narrow focus, which calls into the question the potential effect that this action can have. Does it really represent the reality of the European picture, or is the decision to focus on firms with more than 500 employees a message from the E.U, that they see the catalyst for change coming from the very top? It is hard to tell.

It is difficult to be overly positive about this action from the E.U., despite it being labelled as an important incremental step by some.[54] As Baret and Helrich articulate:

> Of course, despite all these measures, a certain information asymmetry remains: the reporting is inevitably incomplete (even if the company does its best to elaborate its reporting in the most honest and scrupulous way, the indicators can't comprehend the whole set of non-financial aspects and the assessment of some points is still questionable), most stakeholders do not read non-financial documents, those who do not necessary have the skills to analyse them. Moreover, a good number of stakeholders do not

> dedicate themselves to this task of "control" because, contrary to the shareholder, in the "standard" principal-agent pattern, they don't have effective power over the manager to defend their interests. They can, of course, organise themselves on associations, rely on existing NGOs, resort to the public authorities or to the media. But this implies, beyond agency costs, costs in coordination between "weak" stakeholders, and then transaction costs.[55]

For the E.U., the focus has been on testing the water for the initiative with the marketplace. It will be updating the Directive in 2021 and the market has been having its say on the aims of the Directive. Of concern is the scope of the Directive, with respondents to the E.U. expressing concern over the idea of requiring for new topics to be reported on; the fear is one based on over-reporting, and too many requests for information from organisations like CSSs and credit rating agencies. There is strong support for increasing the scope of the Directive to firms with less than 500 employees, non-listed companies, as well as large companies that are established in the E.U. but listed elsewhere.

However, the biggest issue of them all is comparability and standardisation. As the ICAEW report:

> Most respondents concur that there are problems with the comparability, reliability and relevance of non-financial information. The sentiment is particularly high amongst users, with more than 80% finding that limited comparability is a significant issue.
>
> The NFRD does not mandate use of a non-financial reporting standard or framework. There is strong support for this to change, with 82% agreeing that mandating use of a common standard would address key shortcomings. A similar number also favour the inclusion of sector-specific elements in a reporting standard.[56]

The E.U. see the increasing digitisation of information as a pathway to moving these issues along, with the acknowledged administrative burdens that come with mandated non-financial disclosure hopefully being negated, somewhat, as a result.[57]

Nevertheless, it is massively questionable as to whether the E.U. will achieve its objectives with this Directive. What was billed as a vital component of the bloc's future appears to be a watered-down attempt at promoting the concept of non-financial disclosure. One wonders whether there was even a need for this directive, with a lot of companies already publishing such data, albeit not being directly instructed to explain which standards they were using; if that was the outcome of this Directive, was it all worth it? The market is continuing to call for a standard to be imposed, but I wonder how possible this in reality; who could be selected? Would their standards be applicable to the range of markets that need the standards? Would the market respect the choice enforced upon them? Would the E.U. be held accountable for any failures of the standard-setter chosen? Would the E.U. have the capacity or authority to develop their own standards and remove the competitive nature of the private standard-setting business? Would the U.S. approach of preserving the supremacy of the private order conflict with this too much, so much so that the E.U. would inherently have its authority questioned? As we can see, there are more questions than answers in relation to this Directive which one would assume was not the E.U.'s intention.

What is clear is that the European regulatory environment presents a number of challenges and requirements from the CSS and CRA industries, but also presents a wealth of opportunity. Under the Regulation, market participants need to transmit and demonstrate how they are integrating ESG into the practices, and the two industries can certainly help with that requirement. For the Directive, companies with more than 500 employees (and, judging by the market's response, this may be extended to smaller companies) must also signal their incorporation of the principles of sustainability and ESG to the market. It is the required act of signalling, as we saw in the last Chapter, which provides the two industries with their greatest opportunity for relevance and growth, and the E.U. is seemingly marching towards a position whereby the market needs to be informed about what could very well be complicated and complex information. It will need to be simplified. It is within that juncture that the two industries will see their opportunity.

With both the American and European approaches considered, what is the impact on the CSS and credit rating agencies? How do these differing environments affect their trajectories with regard to serving the mainstream investor base? The two approaches will certainly impact the two industries, and we shall now see a number of potential scenarios for the two protagonists in our story.

6.4 'To the Victor Go the Spoils'

There are a number of themes presented in this book that may indicate which industry may be better positioned to serve the mainstream investor base. Nobody has yet declared that these two industries are in competition with each other, but hopefully at this late stage in the book the potential for this conflict is clear. First, the investor base has been clear in what it wants, and also in confirming—alongside an ever-growing body of research—that the CSSs are not yet up to the job. At the same time, the credit rating agencies have been aligning themselves with the sustainable investment movement more and more, and via a number of acquisitions are steadily becoming a major player in the informational services sector in relation to the movement. In the last chapter, we saw how the credit rating agencies are perhaps the ideal vehicle for the investor base because of their oligopolistic organisational model, and their ability to 'signal' better than any CSS. The simple observation that the realm of sustainable investment is becoming more important by the day, but that there is currently no third-party industry that truly suits its needs, leads us to the conclusion that with regard to the CSS and credit rating agencies, two will not go into one; the investors and issuers want *less* choice paradoxically, not more. Perhaps the main question is whether the credit rating agencies would add to their business model to provide the style of ESG information, alongside their ratings, that the market wants. The third chapter makes this question one of the easier questions to answer.

In looking at the regulatory environments earlier in this chapter, we saw the external factors that may influence the direction of this market. Both advantage the CSS and credit rating industries for different reasons, and we shall look at those reasons now. However, before that it is worth looking at any other factors that may affect the potential development of these industries.

6.4.1 *One Last Attempt at Standardisation?*

There can be no doubt that standardisation is *the* main issue in this field. Every investor who is interviewed or surveyed says exactly the same thing. Whilst the sentiment behind the many organisations who have tried to rise to this challenge is admirable, the result has been to make the problem worse. It is simply not possible for there to be a multifaceted response to this request from the market; they want, essentially, a monopolistic governing of the concept of sustainable investing and ESG moreover. There will be many who, rightly or wrongly, argue that the market should not necessarily dictate the direction of this issue, because there needs to be a more holistic vision set out to which the market should aim for. There are a number of very well-articulated arguments against the mainstreamisation of the concept of sustainable investing anyway, and perhaps any more bending to the market's will is inappropriate. After all, whilst the investment banks, credit rating agencies, insurers, mortgage lenders, and a number of other entities took part in the Financial Crisis, the investors gobbled up these toxic securities. They were always supposed to consider the credit rating agencies' ratings as an additional element to their own risk assessments, not a green light for a free-for-all. They themselves should be part of the movement to change practices fundamentally, not just in name only.

However, this argument does not get one very far. Those arguments are still being confined to the niche sectors of ethical investing and that is because, quite simply, *sustainable investing* is something quite different. Sustainable investing involves the mainstream investor base changing their approaches, however slightly. To do that, they will need things on their terms, with their positions and nuances considered at all times. Standardisation is therefore key, because it allows them to integrate the often-subjective elements of ESG into their processes. Those processes often have to be defended because they are representative of more than one can see; a pension fund, for example, may hold the futures of millions of people in their hands so any unnecessary risk is simply not an option. The risk has to be as quantifiable, but more importantly *defendable*, as it can be. To that end, we have seen that this is where the focus is now from a number of organisations, initiatives, and even countries and regions. I will talk about the potential impact of the U.S. and E.U. developments next, but first there is one last private initiative that is worth talking about because it has the real potential to be successful. So much so, it may be the last private hope the market has.

The International Financial Reporting Standards (IFRS) organisation is a standard-setter for the accounting and audit sector and is widely applied. Its standards are utilised around the world, with perhaps only the U.S. being a notable exception (the U.S. GAAP—Generally Accepted Accounting Principles—is used in the U.S., developed by the Financial Accounting Services Board [FASB]). There has consistently been talk of the SEC adopting the IFRS principles, but that has proven to be difficult to accomplish. Nevertheless, the E.U. did adopt the principles and that has led to a near global adoption of the principles. This experience has led to many suggesting that the IFRS could be the organisation to finally bring real standardisation to the sustainability/ESG marketplace and in September of 2020, the IFRS began to answer that call.

In a consultation paper the IFRS published entitled *Consultation Paper on Sustainability Reporting* (with comments to be received by 31st December 2020), the IFRS started by stating that:

> The Trustee Task Force has informally engaged with a cross section of stakeholders involved in sustainability reporting (including the investor and preparer communities, central banks, regulators, public policy makers, auditing firms and other service providers). Through that informal engagement it became clear that sustainability reporting is continuing to increase in importance for those stakeholders. Notwithstanding differences in scope and motivation, all stakeholders share a common message: there is an urgent need to improve the consistency and comparability in sustainability reporting. A set of comparable and consistent standards will allow businesses to build public trust through greater transparency of their sustainability initiatives, which will be helpful to investors and an even broader audience in a context in which society is demanding initiatives to combat climate change...
>
> There have been several recent calls for the IFRS Foundation to become involved in reducing the level of complexity and achieving greater consistency in sustainability reporting. Such calls suggest that the IFRS Foundation's track record and expertise in standard-setting, and its relationships with global regulators and governments around the world, could be useful for setting sustainability reporting standards.[58]

The IFRS went through three options: maintain the status quo, facilitate existing initiatives, or create a 'Sustainability Standards Board' that will seek to build upon other standard-setters work but eventually incorporate as many as possible into one standard. They decided on the idea of a Sustainability Standards Board (SSB) and have painted a picture of it for the market to comment on. The SSB would initially be focused on climate risk, but would eventually aim to incorporate the wider ESG focus. One of the key aims to the idea is to pair the SSB with the IASB (International Accounting Standards Board)—the equivalent for financial reporting—so that there would be an inherent interconnectedness to the two; this could be a particularly important factor for the market.

In order for the IFRS to further develop this plan, it has laid out a number of requirements for success which it says must be met before any further actions are taken. They are:

- Achieving a sufficient level of global support from public authorities, global regulators and market stakeholders, including investors and preparers, in key markets;
- Working with regional initiatives to achieve global consistency and reduce complexity in sustainability reporting;
- Ensuring the adequacy of the governance structure;
- Achieving appropriate technical expertise for the Trustees, SSB members and staff;
- Achieving the level of separate funding required and the capacity to obtain financial support;
- Developing a structure and culture that seeks to build effective synergies with financial reporting; and
- Ensuring the current mission and resources of the IFRS Foundation are not compromised.[59]

Leading figures from the market have responded that this potential of the IFRS entering into the fray could be a 'major breakthrough'.[60] One of the IFRS Trustees said that whilst the IFRS 'are aware of the enormity of the task of developing a global set of sustainability standards', there is 'hope for a new paradigm'.[61] There is clearly a lot of excitement about what could be a game-changer for the marketplace.

We await the publication of the responses to the consultation. There are some issues that may become sticking points, with the first and obvious one being that starting only with a focus on climate risk means that a. a global standard for ESG integration will not be forthcoming anytime soon, and b. this just adds another voice to the cacophony of noise in the marketplace already. The IFRS do say that 'the Task Force's research and informal consultation indicates that developing global sustainability-reporting standards for climate-related information is the most pressing concern', and this is understandable. The pressure to adhere with the Paris Agreement is intense, and the suspected reintegration of the U.S. into the agreement once the Biden Administration takes over will only add to the pressure on the market. Perhaps then the IFRS is right to focus on one element first and get it right, but the point still stands that a global standard-setter is still not in effect via this IFRS plan. Yet, on the other key issues such as defining materiality and then what processes may be put in place for assurance, the IFRS is particularly vague. Perhaps it is too early in the process to hold them to account, but the lack of information even about how they may plan to focus on these issues is worrying.

Therefore, the IFRS potentially represents the last chance for a private solution to the issues affecting the marketplace. There are holes in the plan, but the plan is still very much afloat. The IFRS has the potential to knit together the globally disparate framework for reporting standards and truly set forth a path that market participants will follow, and that alone is promising. The next stages of the plan are perhaps the most important because it will be the details that bring the market along for the ride.

6.4.2 *What the Sustainability Environment Means for the CSS and Credit Rating Industries*

If standardisation is the main aspect affecting the progression of the mainstreamisation of sustainable investing, then what does that mean for the CSS and credit rating agencies? I argue that it is *the* defining element. Simply put, I argue at this stage of the book that whoever fits the mainstream investors' needs best will eventually go on to fundamentally attach itself to this soon-to-be norm. There are few scenarios that may come to bear which could impact upon how the industries progress.

- The E.U. succeeds in increasing the standardisation across non-financial disclosure—if the E.U. succeeds in its mission, then it will go a long way to fixing one of the major defences from the CSSs regarding their failure to meet the market's demands so far: they do not have access to all the information they need to make the ratings/rankings that investors are asking for. If this informational flow is increased and the CSSs' accuracy and relevance increases, then the CSSs could enjoy greater successes. This would leave the CSSs needing to form a more oligopolistic industrial model, or even setting standards across their own industry for the benefit of its end users—the investors. However, if the informational flow does increase but the CSSs continue to be sporadic with their accuracy and relevance, then the market would be left with no alternative but to look elsewhere for its ESG ratings/rankings.

- Institutional Investors in the U.S. step and succeed in pushing issuers to disclose better and more standardised information—if the approach of allowing the market to be made by institutional investors pays off, then the same effect as the European scenario above would be witnessed. The same outcome then applies, leaving the CSSs with nowhere to go if the relevancy of their products does not increase.
- The IFRS roll out their SSB, and it massively increases the standardisation in the market—if the IFRS decide to move forward with their SSB proposal, and it succeeds, the increase in the standardisation of information would pile real pressure on the CSS universe, because then the misalignment with the investors' needs would come from the CSSs and their models, not the market. However, if the CSSs can organise effectively and the ESG information in the market becomes more standardised, then they could just as easily profit handsomely.
- The CSS universe becomes smaller—One aspect that could easily change is that the CSS universe becomes a lot smaller, with the larger players integrating the array of smaller players so that an oligopoly is formed. Just like the natural pressures that form expensive stones, there are a number of external pressures currently affecting the CSS universe that could produce an oligopolistic model. If the larger players like MSCI and Refinitiv turn their attention to reducing the competition in the market, then the investor base would potentially be more satisfied with less options—particularly if there is an increased informational flow and standardisation being funnelled through the new oligopoly.
- The credit rating agencies turn their attention to the CSS universe—admittedly, there is not much left to acquire, but there are enough players left in the CSS universe to result in the need for a concerted acquisition strategy from the credit rating oligopoly. There are a few issues with this suggestion though. First, S&P's proposed purchase of IHS Markit for $44 billion potentially suggests that the leading agencies do not have the appetite for the CSS market at present, more the data services markets. Also, there are not many market leaders to acquire; Refinitiv is in the crosshairs of the London Stock Exchange, and MSCI is likely out of reach, or at least the spinning off of their ESG services. But, the rating agencies could easily acquire the fringes of the CSS market, although that leaves the risk of leaving a de facto oligopoly in place which could compete for the lucrative market forming for ESG ratings/rankings.

- The credit rating agencies merely start offering the same as the CSSs—this is already the case in truth. But, if the credit rating agencies continue down the path they have set with the branded ESG integrative products, then what need is there for the CSSs? If the credit rating agencies continue to integrate the specialisms of the smaller players they are purchasing (like Moody's and Vigeo-Eiris), then the market may just simply turn to the credit rating agencies because of the practical relevancy of their industrial model.

Ultimately, these are all hypothetical with some more realistic than others. What is for sure is that whoever ends up efficiently aligning themselves to the movement will reap the rewards. Essentially, there are some realisms that need to be applied. The first is that E.U. is unlikely to succeed in its mission, purely because of the softness of its approach; mandating that market participants must inform the market of what standards they are using is not enough and merely peels back one layer of the onion. The second is that the U.S. approach of encouraging institutional investors to push for change will only ever go so far, and that will be nowhere near enough. Not only does it place the responsibility on a handful of investors who have historically not been very active, but there exist so many legal protections for the issuers that the chances of true change are very slim; if we add to this the tone of the political tensions within the country, one cannot be hopeful. The IFRS represent a really exciting potential, but that is all it is so far. There is a massive amount of detail missing within their plans, and what we do know is that they will be taking an incremental approach to building ESG-related standards; change will not come overnight, if at all. Third, if the CSSs start devouring each other, there is a good chance that the development of an oligopolistic model might save their industry and make them relevant to the investor base that will dictate their future. However, if the smaller CSSs start being acquired, then it is more likely that the incredibly well-resourced credit rating agencies will be the ones doing the devouring. If the credit rating agencies continue on their course, they will have devoured the CSS universe in due time. That would leave only the largest players in the CSS universe, which could potentially create an opposing oligopoly, but the likelihood is that the leading CSSs would focus on different markets, like that for indexes, etc. The credit rating industry is, rightly or wrongly, perfect for the investor base and, ultimately, the mainstreamisation of the sustainable investing concept.

I feel that it is very important, as we conclude this book, that it is made abundantly clear that this conclusion that the credit rating agencies are more likely to be the victor is not based on their performance. The credit rating agencies' failure in the Financial Crisis was breathtaking and, whilst it may be belittled by some, I argue that the Financial Crisis was built upon the transgressions of the credit rating industry; without their involvement it simply would not have been possible. Therefore, this suggestion is not that they *should* be aligned to the development of the movement, more that they *will*. Their model is perfect. Their products are already generally standardised, which suggests that their transmission of the effects of ESG would be so too. They all present slightly varying versions of the same information and are known for converging. They are also well known for catering to their market. But, more than anything, *they* are widely known. The market knows the credit rating agencies, what they do, and how they do it. This is a commodity that the CSSs do not have, and it is worth its weight in (sustainably mined!) gold. The credit rating agencies would be willing partners in the development of the mainstreamisation of sustainable investment, which itself is a novel concept because it is far away from what traditional understandings of responsible investment have been. The marriage of the mainstreamisation of the concept and the credit rating agencies is a natural one. There is also the potential that the oligopolistic model, if it can become comfortable with any potential exposure to liability (which it will not be!), can start to form common understandings of what 'materiality' is in this sector, and what it means to be 'sustainable'. It is more likely that a private standard-setter like the IFRS will do this because of the lack of liability they would be exposed to as opposed to the credit rating agencies, but the potential is still there via their commentaries and support for their products.

It is perhaps a sour ending to the book to say that the true integration of ESG into modern and mainstream investment practices is some way off. There is not even agreement on what it should look like, what counts as material, or how that information should be disclosed. Regrettably, the good intentions of many are making the problem worse. The only way to achieve quantifiable success in this arena is to let the financial powerhouses morph the meaning of the concept to their needs. Perhaps this is no success at all, or equally the greatest success in the post-Crisis world. If market participants can become even incrementally more responsible in their practices, then surely that is a positive response to the Crisis? But, what does that do to the concept of true responsible investing? Does the development of the mainstream space kill the fringe? If so, the narrative will be fundamentally changed by the corporate space that it was supposed to dictate to, not be dictated by. What I can guarantee is that the credit rating agencies will not suffer because of this connection—they will make it work for them; doing so is in their cultural DNA. Understanding this, based on understanding their cultural identity as developed since the 1840s, means that the 'battle' between the CSSs and the credit rating agencies was never even a 'battle' to begin with, merely a process to a predictable end.

Notes

1. For different perspectives on this ecological disaster, see P.G. Wells, James N. Butler, and Jane S. Hughes, *Exxon Valdez Oil Spill: Fate and Effects in Alaskan Waters* (ASTM International 1995).
2. Kathleen H. Rupley, Darrell Brown, and Scott Marshall, 'Evolution of Corporate Reporting: From Stand-Alone Corporate Social Responsibility Reporting to Integrated Reporting' (2017) 29 *Research in Accounting Regulation* 172–176, 173.
3. Susanne Arvidsson, 'An Expose of the Challenging Practice Development of Sustainability Reporting: From the First Wave to the EU Directive (2014/95/EU)' in Susanne Arvidsson (ed), *Challenges in Managing Sustainable Business: Reporting, Taxation, Ethics and Governance* (Springer 2018) 12.
4. Ralph Thurm, 'Taking the GRI to Scale' in Stefan Schaltegger, Martin Bennett, and Roger Burritt, *Sustainability Accounting and Reporting* (Springer 2006) 326.
5. Seleshi Sisaye, *Ecology, Sustainable Development and Accounting* (Routledge 2015) 103.
6. (n 3).
7. Christophe Revelli, 'Socially Responsible Investing (SRI): From Mainstream to Margin?' (2017) 39 *Research in International Business and Finance* 711–717, 715.
8. Christophe Revelli, 'Socially Responsible Investment (SRI): Meta-Debate and Development Perspectives' in Bernard Paranque and Roland Perez, *Finance Reconsidered: New Perspectives for a Responsible and Sustainable Finance* (Emerald 2016) 166.
9. Ruth Jebe, 'The Convergence of Financial and ESG Materiality: Taking Sustainability Mainstream' (2019) 56 *American Business Law Journal* 3 645–702, 682.
10. Zabihollah Rezaee, *Business Sustainability, Corporate Governance, and Organisational Ethics* (John Wiley & Sons 2019) 260.

11. Jody Grewal, Clarissa Hauptmann, and George Serafeim, 'Material Sustainability Information and Stock Price Informativeness' (2020) *Journal of Business Ethics* (Published Online Feb 11) 2.
12. (n 10).
13. Cristiano Busco, Costanza Consolandi, Robert G. Eccles, and Elena Sofra, 'A Preliminary Analysis of SASB Reporting: Disclosure Topics, Financial Relevance, and the Financial Intensity of ESG Materiality' (2020) 32 *Journal of Applied Corporate Finance* 2 117, 119.
14. Ibid.
15. Robert G. Eccles, Linda-Eling Lee, and Judith C. Stroehle, 'The Social Origins of ESG: An Analysis of Innovest and KLD' (2019) *Organization & Environment* 1–22, 5.
16. Virginia H. Ho, 'Non-financial Reporting & Corporate Governance: Explaining American Divergence & Its Implications for Disclosure Reform' (2020) *Accounting, Economics, and Law: A Convivium* 1–29, 2.
17. Virginia H. Ho, 'From Public Policy to Materiality: Non-financial Reporting, Shareholder Engagement, and Rule 14a-8's Ordinary Business Exception' (2019) 76 *Washington and Lee Law Review* 3 1231–1257, 1243.
18. Ibid 1252.
19. Virginia Harper Ho, 'Disclosure Overload? Lessons for Risk Disclosure & ESG Reporting Reform from the Regulation S-K Concept Release' (2020) 65 *Villanova Law Review* 67–133, 70.
20. Jill E Fisch, 'Making Sustainability Disclosure Sustainable' (2019) 107 *The Georgetown Law Journal* 923–966, 928.
21. ibid 80.
22. World Business Council for Sustainable Development, *The Reporting Exchange: Corporate Reporting in the United States and Canada* (WBCSD 2018) 4.
23. (n 17) 1243.
24. US Chamber Foundation, *Corporate Sustainability: Past, Present, and Future* (2018) https://www.uschamberfoundation.org/sites/default/files/Corporate%20Sustainability%20Reporting%20Past%20Present%20Future.pdf 26.
25. Virginia Harper Ho, 'Nonfinancial Risk Disclosure and the Costs of Private Ordering' (2018) 55 *American Business Law Journal* 3 407–474, 432.
26. Ibid 429.
27. (n 24) 9.
28. Ibid.
29. (n 20) 934.

30. Joel Seligman, 'The SEC's Unfinished Soft Information Revolution' (1995) 63 *Fordham Law Review* 6 1955.
31. (n 20) 935.
32. (n 17) 1253.
33. John C. Coffee, 'The Future of Disclosure: ESG, Common Ownership, and Systemic Risk' (2020) *European Corporate Governance Institute: Law Working Paper No. 541/2020* https://scholarship.law.columbia.edu/cgi/viewcontent.cgi?article=3684&context=faculty_scholarship 26.
34. (n 19) 131.
35. Jessica DiNapoli and Ross Kerber, 'Labor Department Finalises U.S. Rule Curbing Sustainable Investing by Pension Funds' (2020) *Reuters* (Oct 30) https://uk.reuters.com/article/us-esg-rule/labor-department-finalizes-u-s-rule-curbing-sustainable-investing-by-pension-funds-idUKKBN27F35M (Accessed 02/01/21).
36. Gillian Tett, 'Investors Should Watch the Transatlantic Split on ESG Closely' (2020) *Financial Times* (Oct 15) https://www.ft.com/content/3ea99abb-d709-4d1f-ab23-56aed7f34c90 (Accessed 02/02/21).
37. BBC, '*EU Budget Blocked by Hungary and Poland Over Rule of Law Issue*' (2020) https://www.bbc.co.uk/news/world-europe-54964858 (Accessed 02/01/21).
38. For an Extensive Review of the Threats Facing the Bloc See Desmond Dinan, Neill Nugent, and William E. Peterson, *The European Union in Crisis* (Macmillan 2017).
39. Selena Aureli, Elisabetta Magnaghi, and Federica Salvatori, 'The Role of Existing Regulation and Discretion in Harmonising Non-Financial Disclosure' (2019) 16 *Accounting in Europe* 3 290–312, 293.
40. Fabian Hertel, *Effective Internal Control and Corporate Compliance: A Law and Economics Impact Analysis of the Mysteries of a German Aktiengesellschaft Listed on the NYSE* (Nomos Verlag) 263.
41. Regulation (EU) 2019/2088 of the European Parliament and of the Council on Sustainability-Related Disclosures in the Financial Services Sector.
42. Danny Busch, 'Sustainable Finance Disclosure in the EU Financial Sector (2020) 70 *EBI Working Paper Series*.
43. Directive 2014/95/EU of the European Parliament and of the Council, Amending Directive 2013/34/EU as Regards Disclosure of Non-financial and Diversity Information by Certain Large Undertakings and Groups.
44. Georgina Tsagas and Charlotte Villiers, 'Why "Less Is More" in Non-financial Reporting Initiatives: Concrete Steps Towards Supporting Sustainability' (2020) 10 *Accounting, Economics, and Law: A Convivium* 2, 20.
45. The European Commission, *Types of EU Law* (2021) https://ec.europa.eu/info/law/law-making-process/types-eu-law_en (Accessed 02/01/21).

46. (n 39) 291.
47. Gregory Jackson, Julia Bartosch, Emma Avetisyan, Daniel Kinderman, and Jette Steen Knudsen, 'Mandatory Non-financial Disclosure and Its Influence on CSR: An International Comparison' (2020) 162 *Journal of Business Ethics* 323–42, 325.
48. (n 44) 21.
49. Ibid 23.
50. (n 44) 23.
51. (n 39) 292.
52. (n 47) 334.
53. Francesco De Luca, *Mandatory and Discretional Non-financial Disclosure After the European Directive 2014/95/EU: An Empirical Analysis of Italian-Based Companies' Behaviour* (Emerald 2020) 76.
54. (n 44) 34.
55. Pierre Baret and Vincent Helrich, 'The "Trilemma" of Non-financial Reporting and Its Pitfalls' (2018) 23 *Journal of Management and Governance* 485–511, 495.
56. ICAEW '*European Companies Support Non-financial Reporting Rule Changes*' (2020) https://www.icaew.com/insights/viewpoints-on-the-news/2020/aug-2020/european-companies-support-nonfinancial-reporting-rule-changes (Accessed 02/02/21).
57. The Report Summarising the Responses – European Union, *Summary Report of the Public Consultation on the Review of the Non-Financial Reporting Directive* (Ares(2020)3,997,889) 42.
58. IFRS, *Consultation Paper on Sustainability Reporting* (IFRS 2020) https://cdn.ifrs.org/-/media/project/sustainability-reporting/consultation-paper-on-sustainability-reporting.pdf (Accessed 03/01/21).
59. ibid 9.
60. Susanna Rust, '"Breakthrough" as IFRS Body Proposes Sustainability Standards Board' (2020) IPE (Sept. 30) https://www.ipe.com/news/breakthrough-as-ifrs-body-proposes-sustainability-standards-board/10048161.article (Accessed 03/01/21).
61. IFRS, '*Hope for a New Paradigm – Sustainability Reporting*' (2020) https://www.ifrs.org/news-and-events/2020/10/hope-for-a-new-paradigm-sustainability-reporting/ (Accessed 03/02/21).

CHAPTER 7

Conclusion

In the prophesised battle between the two industries, we can now see that unless something external and unexpected happens, the likely winner was always the favourite. There are so many factors that could affect the progression of this market and a significant amount of those favour the credit rating agencies. As was stated in the last chapter, this is not through performance but merely because of the function of the credit rating agencies; their model fits best.

What the oligopolistic credit rating model fits best is the mainstreamisation of the concept of sustainable investment. This 'mainstreamisation' is a concept that needs to be considered at all times, because as we saw it fundamentally impacts the rules of the game. The development must be on the terms of the world's leading investors, otherwise they have very little incentive to partake; it is the world that needs their involvement, not them. Whilst the vast majority have publicly stated that they see the value in integrating ESG into their practices, they will just as easily be able to make money without doing so faithfully. Scholars concerned with the true development of responsible and ethical investing somewhat lament the mainstreamisation, which is understandable. However, to potentially move the mainstream away from solely considering just financial-related issues will be a remarkable feat if it is achieved.

It will be remarkable solely because of the challenges that have to be overcome. The insistence of the Trump Administration that ESG will not

D. Cash, *Sustainability Rating Agencies vs Credit Rating Agencies*, Palgrave Studies in Impact Finance,
https://doi.org/10.1007/978-3-030-71693-6_7

be considered by Trustees of large institutional investors—so much so they banned pension funds from considering ESG, which in itself is truly remarkable and not consistent with the U.S.'s laissez-fair economic attitude—is just one extreme example of the challenges facing the concept. We saw that the largest hurdle by far was the need to standardise. This is because within that concept there are so many elements that need to be considered, like agreeing on an understanding of what a 'material' ESG risk looks like, when it may come into effect, and for how long. The wide variety of ESG issues, and the wider still application of those issues to the diverse market place, is proving a humungous hurdle to clear. What is needed is market-based authority, which not many have. The E.U. is currently finding that it does not have the authority to impose upon the market which standard it needs to consider, and the ever-changing geopolitical landscape means that no country is likely able to impose such an approach either. The U.N. initiatives are also finding the same issue. This is because the market is not often dictated to when there is so much subjectivity at play, but also because in promoting one standard over another, the exposure to liability and blame is a real concern.

It is for this reason that there are two potential developments that I predict may move the movement in a rapidly new direction. The IFRS's plan to build a sustainability board is arguably the best hope the market has now for developing and establishing some standards in the market that will be adhered to. The IFRS has the market-based authority to: a. bring together the vast number of standard-setters who are creating 'noise' in this arena, and then b. dictate it to the market; its performance in setting accounting-based standards gives it the experience and the acceptance an ultimate standard-setter needs in this arena. However, it so early in this process for the IFRS that it is impossible to predict whether it will be successful or not (or even launched at this point!) Nevertheless, in principle, it is an exciting development. Another market-based entity that could lead on this development is the credit rating agencies themselves. If they start to build ESG research-related products more than what they are doing, which I predict they will, then they have the potential to define elements such as 'materiality', and in communicating this with the market they could, essentially, 'make the market'. The most obvious reason why they will not do this is because it forces them to stick their neck out and expose themselves to liability from the market. The credit rating agencies detest liability, so this is not the most likely scenario. However, they do have a 'market licence' to operate and their performance, whether good or bad, bears very little reflection on their ability to exist and prosper.

What is for sure is that the CSS universe is under considerable pressure. The largest operators—MSCI and Refinitiv—are largely safe because they are huge entities and have diversified product ranges. But, for the smaller CSSs, they are directly in the crosshairs of the credit rating agencies and it is just a matter of time before you hear of one of the CSSs identified in Chapter 2 being sold to a leading credit rating agency. The development of an oligopoly in the CSS industry could be beneficial to the market place, but the CSS oligopoly would lack the history and visibility of the credit rating oligopoly; perhaps they are more important factors than I have given them credit for.

The battle for the mainstream investor may not be obvious, but it is already underway. At this stage, the CSSs are under siege. The mainstream investor base is tentative, and onlooking scholars and journalists are continuing to identify flaws in their offering. What can turn that tide? It is difficult to say. The credit rating agencies, though, are not waiting to find out if they can achieve it. They are purposively and consciously turning their attention to the ESG marketplace and making sure that the fact they have some of the highest profitability ratios in the world works in their favour. Though not a CSS, the forthcoming takeover of IHS Markit by S&P for $44bn is a statement to everybody; the credit rating agencies have the resources and they will use them for their benefit. It is almost certain that Moody's will respond in kind at some point, and if they decide to consider the CSS universe instead of just the data provider industry that is currently the hottest ticket in town, the battle could be over before most realise it had even begun. The credit rating agencies are a locomotive, and one wonders whether the CSS industry is tied to the tracks. Time will tell.

Index

D. Cash, *Sustainability Rating Agencies vs Credit Rating Agencies*, Palgrave Studies in Impact Finance,
https://doi.org/10.1007/978-3-030-71693-6

The manufacturer's authorised representative in the EU is Springer Nature Customer Service Centre GmbH, Europaplatz 3, 69115 Heidelberg, Germany. If you have any concerns regarding our products, please contact ProductSafety@springernature.com

Printed and bound by CPI Group (UK) Ltd, Croydon, CR0 4YY
30/09/2026
02225711-0004